**Easy Chinese Readings**

# LIFE IN BEIJING

生活在北京

SERIES EDITOR
**Jian Zhu**

AUTHOR
**Qingsheng Ma**

This book will
quickly increase your ability to read Chinese

**BIGI**

# Copyright

**Life in Beijing**

Copyright 1998 © BIGI International USA Inc.

All rights reserved. No part of this book may be reproduced or transmitted in any form or by any means, electronic or mechanical, including photocopying, recording or by any information storage or retrieval system, without written permission from the publisher, except for the inclusion of brief quotations in a review.

ISBN 1-891107-02-X

Library of Congress Card Catalog Number     97-074382

First Edition

Written and Edited by Jian Zhu
Translated by Molly Luethi
Cover and text design by Fong-Zhen Shiao
Cover illustration by Shih-Lun Tang
Chapter graphics by Carol Baldwin / Shih-Lun Tang / Chih-Hsiung Chien

**Purchases, Inquiries, or Suggestions:**
BIGI International USA Inc.

**ChineseBridge Publishing Ltd.**
34, Foxwood Drive
Port Moody, B.C.
Canada  V3H 4X3
Tel: 1-604-469-1456

Printed in Taiwan

# Preface

<u>Life in Beijing</u> is one text in a series of innovative new Chinese readers written and edited specifically for students of Chinese who have had intensive beginning instruction (or the equivalent of four semesters of Chinese studies), and want to quickly improve their reading, writing, and speaking skills.

These books have been designed to help readers with fluency and proficiency within a format of rich cultural content aimed at providing readers with a greater understanding of the Chinese culture. The texts span a number of compelling topics ranging from ancient stories and traditions to current lifestyles and social change. We know of no other textbooks on the market encompassing such variety of topics and written in contemporary, up-to-date Chinese.

Readers of this series are presumed to have learned 500 basic characters from which to work. Unfortunately, when many students of Chinese have gained this level of competency, there are few materials to read to help them maintain their vocabulary and improve their reading skills. Our books have been written with careful attention to characters, expressions, grammar, and sentence structure to help readers achieve greater fluency. Cumbersome notes and explanations are unnecessary to understand the grammar in this series.

In addition to fluency, these texts are intended to help readers increase their vocabulary and use of common expressions. Each lesson contains approximately twenty to thirty new expressions for readers to learn. Some of these expressions may not be completely new, however, because they are combinations of characters readers already know, enabling readers to increase their vocabulary from chapter to chapter. For example, while readers will have already learned the characters for "big" and "person," when combined in the new expression as "big person," readers then learn the expression for "adult." There are hundreds of such examples in these books, as well as numerous current expressions now used in contemporary China.

One of the most powerful tools of language learning is repetition. Editors have worked diligently to ensure that these textbooks contain just the right amount of repetition of expressions and sentence structures. While these repetitions may at times appear redundant or excessive, many of these expressions are used frequently by the Chinese on a daily basis, and readers should gain a sense of their importance and variety of usage.

Readers' increased fluency and proficiency in Chinese is the editors' goal. We have also strived to produce books which make the study of Chinese both interesting and meaningful. Additional titles to enrich cultural understanding and language proficiency include <u>Chinese Myths and Folktales</u> and <u>Chinese Traditions and Festivals</u>, both of which are in our series, **<u>Easy Chinese Readings in 500 Characters</u>**.

# 本書序言

  <u>生活在北京</u>是"**以五百生字輕鬆閱讀中文**"系列叢書中的一本。這一系列中文閱讀叢書是為**受過初步漢語訓練**（相當於經過四個學期的中文課程學習），並希望迅速提高閱讀中文能力的學生而編寫的。

  為了使讀者更深更廣地了解中國文化，從而使讀者熟練掌握中文，這一系列叢書提供了讀者眾多而有趣的文章，以介紹豐富的中國文化。文章主題和內容十分廣泛，從中國的古代傳說和習俗，到現代的生活方式及社會變化。據我們所知，目前書市上還看不到涵蓋如此廣泛的主題，而且使用當代中文表達的教科書，可以滿足這一讀者群的需要。

  這一系列叢書假定讀者有五百個中文生字的基礎，即可以開始閱讀這一系列叢書。雖然現在有許多學生有五百字的中文能力，但不幸的是沒有可供他們閱讀的文章，以幫助他們維持已經學到的生字，並提高閱讀能力。我們向您推薦的這一系列叢書，其生字、習慣用語、語法和句子結構都經過仔細地推敲，使學生可以流暢閱讀。其中文章的文法簡單易懂，沒有加冗長的注釋或解釋的必要。

  除了其流暢性之外，這些文章的一個特點是：迅速增加讀者的詞彙量，並使他們熟悉日常的中文習慣表達法。每一課文章包含了大約二十到三十個讀者應該學習的新詞彙。它們並不是全新的詞彙，它們都是由讀者已經熟悉的字組成的。舉例來說，如讀者已經認識"大"和"人"兩個字，將這兩個字組合起來就成了"大人"這個詞。這樣的詞彙在文章中，讀者就可以很容易學會並加大其詞彙量。這些書中不但有數百個這樣的例子，而且還包含了許許多多現代中國人正在使用的習慣表達法。就這樣，使讀者能夠逐課並迅速地增加詞彙量。

  重複是學習語言的最有效的工具之一。編輯們努力使一些習慣用語和句子結構在書中有恰到好處的多次重複。雖然有些重複的地方顯得多餘，但這些被重複的習慣用語，卻是中國人經常時用的。所以，讀者可以從文中體會它們的重要性，並明白它們的多種用法。

  我們努力使讀者熟練掌握中文，同時也努力使文章有實質性的內容，讓讀者產生對中文更深的興趣。像這樣提高讀者文化理解能力和中文熟練程度的書籍，除了本書"<u>生活在北京</u>"之外，我們還有"<u>中國的節日與民俗</u>"以及"<u>中國神話與民間故事</u>"兩本，都屬於這一個"以五百生字輕鬆閱讀中文"的系列叢書。

# CONTENTS

| | | | |
|---|---|---|---|
| *Chapter 1* | Tian An Men - The Gate of Heavenly Peace | ............... | 1 |
| *Chapter 2* | Beijing Opera | ............... | 21 |
| *Chapter 3* | The University of Beijing | ............... | 39 |
| *Chapter 4* | The Forbidden City | ............... | 55 |
| *Chapter 5* | Famous Old Stores and Snack Bars | ............... | 73 |
| *Chapter 6* | The Summer Palace and the Great Wall | ............... | 89 |
| *Chapter 7* | Wang Fu Jing Avenue and Changing Consumerism | ......... | 103 |
| *Chapter 8* | Life in Middle and Elementary Schools | ............... | 117 |
| *Chapter 9* | Holidays in Beijing | ............... | 133 |
| *Chapter 10* | Beijing's Courtyards and Alleys | ............... | 147 |
| *Chapter 11* | Beijing's Night Markets and Its Night Life | ............... | 163 |
| *Chapter 12* | The Kingdom of Bicycles | ............... | 177 |
| *Chapter 13* | Weekend Excursions | ............... | 195 |
| *Chapter 14* | Open Produce Markets and Family Businesses | ............... | 211 |
| *Chapter 15* | The People of Beijing and the Beijing Dialect | ............... | 225 |
| *Chapter 16* | Changing Beijing | ............... | 241 |

# 目錄

第一章　天安門　1
第二章　京劇　21
第三章　北京大學　39
第四章　故宮　55
第五章　北京的老字號和小吃　73
第六章　頤和園和長城　89
第七章　王府井大街和變化中的消費生活　103
第八章　中小學生的學校生活　117
第九章　節日的北京　133
第十章　北京的四合院和胡同　147
第十一章　北京的夜市和夜生活　163
第十二章　自行車的王國　177
第十三章　周末與郊遊　195
第十四章　菜市場和個體戶　211
第十五章　北京人和北京話　225
第十六章　變化中的北京　241

# 第一章　天安門

北京[1]是中國的首都[2]，天安門[3]是首都的象徵[4]。當說到北京的時候，人們第一個想到的就是天安門，天安門原來是北京的一個地方的名字，也是一個門的名字，這個門很大很大，是古時候北京城的一個主要的城門[5]，那時候天安門就好像是皇帝[6]家的大門，站在天安門上可以看得很遠很遠。

天安門的前面有一條小河，是為了保護[7]皇帝的家。所以，這條河也叫護城河[8]，護城河上有一座橋[9]，叫作金水橋[10]。天安門的前面現在是一個很大很大的廣場[11]，叫作天安門廣場。天安門的後面是一座非常大的建築群[12]，那是以前皇帝住的地方，因為那是古時候的皇宮[13]，所以中國人把它叫作"故宮[14]"。

天安門廣場是世界上第二大的廣場，是現代[15]中國的一大奇觀[16]，它在今天中國人心裏是一個非常重要的地方。每天都有許多人來這裏遊覽[17]，他們從中國的四面八方[18]來，從世界的各個國家來。每天早晨，天安門廣場上都會舉行[19]升旗[20]的儀式[21]，天剛剛亮，太陽還沒有升起來的時候，人們就等候[22]在這裏觀看[23]升旗儀式。太陽下山[24]的時候，遊覽的人們又一群一群[25]地等候在這裏，觀看降旗[26]儀式。

每年的十月,是中國的國慶節[27],這個時候,在廣場上會舉行許多的慶祝[28]活動[29],天安門廣場非常地美麗。國旗[30]、紅旗、各種顏色的鮮花[31]和節日的氣球[32]到處都是。穿著漂亮衣服的人們,都會成群地來到這裏一起慶祝。一九四九年的十月一號,中國政府[33]在這裏舉行了第一個國慶節,從那以後[34],每年的這個時候,全中國的人民都一起舉行慶祝活動,天安門就是這個節日的中心。

每一次國家重大的節日,政府都會在這裏舉行活動,國家元首[35]和政府重要的人物[36]都要在天安門的城門上,對天安門廣場上的人群[37]和全中國人民講話[38]。同時,天安門廣場也是中國政府歡迎外國政府來賓[39]的地方,每一次外國元首來中國訪問,中國政府都要在天安門廣場上舉行歡迎儀式和許多活動,歡迎他們到中國來。

廣場的四面都有許多高大且壯觀[40]的建築物,廣場的西面是人民大會堂[41],這裏是國家開大會的地方,每年有許多重要的大會都在這裏舉行。廣場的東面是中國最大的歷史博物館[42],裏面可以看到許多介紹中國歷史的文物[43]。在天安門廣場的附近還有很多重要的政府大樓[44],這些地方也是遊覽的人們常來參觀[45]的地方。

因為天安門廣場上非常大,所以經常有人來這裏放風箏[46],雖然在廣場上可以買到各種好看的風箏,許多北京人還是喜歡自己做的風箏，他們的風箏有的是幾米長[47]，還有的是十幾米長，當然，他們的風箏是做得非常好的。除了冬天和政府有活動的日子[48]，差不多每天你都可以在這裏看到放風箏。許多人來北京，也一定要到天安門廣場來，親眼[49]觀看這個有趣的活動。

八十年代以前，天安門的城門是不讓一般[50]的人上去的。在節日裏，只有政府重要的人物和他們請的客人和朋友才能上去。他們在那裏觀看在廣場上舉行的慶祝活動。到了九十年代，政府才開放天安門，讓人們四處[51]參觀。從那以後，每天都有許多人到天安門城門上，參觀這個古時候皇帝家的大門。到了天安門的上面，你就會明白，當時的皇帝為什麼要建這麼大的城門，你就會知道天安門廣場有多大。

天安門和天安門廣場的中間有一條大街[52]，叫作長安街[53]。你一定很奇怪，為什麼這些名字裏面都有一個"安"字，"安"在中文裏就是平安的意思，中國人認為"安"是一個非常有福的字。長安街是一條北京主要的大街，因為原來的長安街從東到西有十公里長，所以也叫做"十里長街"，長安街的下面是北京的地下[54]鐵道[55]，也叫做地鐵[56]，過去政府不讓地鐵從天安門下面經過[57]，到了九十年代，政府才讓地鐵從長安街下面經過。

天安門廣場的南面是正陽門[58]，正陽門是一座古城門，五十年代以前正陽門還是原來的樣子，在正陽門的兩邊是古城牆，古城牆的裏面就是原來的北京。在古時候，正陽門的古城牆和天安門的古城牆之間住的是一般的老百姓，只有皇帝和皇帝的家人才能住在天安門的裏面，正陽門兩邊的古城牆很長很長，環繞[59]著古時候的北京。這個古城牆一直到五十年代的時候還在。

從五十年代起，政府覺得古城牆裏面的北京太小了，就決定[60]拿走古城牆，結果，政府花了很多的人力和物力[61]把古城牆拿走，並在古城牆的地方建了一條環繞北京的公路，並在這條公路的下面建了一條環繞北京的地鐵。從那以後——特別是經過最近幾十年的變化，北京的樣子和以前大不一樣[62]了，北京的人口[63]也比原來多了許多。

今天的北京已經比原來大多了，不再是原來古城牆裏面的北京了。但是，許多的北京人還是認為古城牆裏面的北京才是真正的北京。雖然，今天的北京與四十多年前的北京很不一樣，政府還是希望保護古時候的建築，所以政府規定在北京不可以建特別高的建築。許多古時候的建築，像故宮，天壇[64]和頤和園[65]政府都特別花人力和物力來保護。這些古建築代表了中國的歷史和文化，在天安門這個地方，你可以觀看到中國的過去和現在；你也可以看見中國的將來。

## 閱讀理解

一、天安門廣場有多大？
二、每天在天安間廣場有什麼儀式？
三、天安門廣場爲什麼這麼重要？
四、廣場前面的大街叫什麼名字？
五、爲什麼天安門的城門不讓一般人上去？
六、爲什麼政府要拿走北京的古城牆？
七、爲什麼政府不讓地鐵從天安門的下面經過？

## 生字

| | | | | |
|---|---|---|---|---|
| 1 | 北京 | běijīng | ㄅㄟˇ ㄐㄧㄥ | Beijing, the capitol of the People's Republic of China |
| 2 | 首都 | shǒudū | ㄕㄡˇ ㄉㄨ | capitol |
| 3 | 天安門 | tiānānmén | ㄊㄧㄢ ㄢ ㄇㄣˊ | The Gate of Heavenly Peace |
| 4 | 象徵 | xiàngzhēng | ㄒㄧㄤˋ ㄓㄥ | symbol |
| 5 | 城門 | chéngmén | ㄔㄥˊ ㄇㄣˊ | city gate |
| 6 | 皇帝 | huángdì | ㄏㄨㄤˊ ㄉㄧˋ | emperor |
| 7 | 保護 | bǎohù | ㄅㄠˇ ㄏㄨˋ | to protect |
| 8 | 護城河 | hùchénghé | ㄏㄨˋ ㄔㄥˊ ㄏㄜˊ | moat |
| 9 | 橋 | qiáo | ㄑㄧㄠˊ | bridge |
| 10 | 金水橋 | jīnshuǐqiáo | ㄐㄧㄣ ㄕㄨㄟˇ ㄑㄧㄠˊ | Golden Bridge |
| 11 | 廣場 | guǎngchǎng | ㄍㄨㄤˇ ㄔㄤˇ | square |
| 12 | 建築群 | jiànzhùqún | ㄐㄧㄢˋ ㄓㄨˋ ㄑㄩㄣˊ | group of buildings |

| | | | | |
|---|---|---|---|---|
| 13 | 皇宮 | huánggōng | ㄏㄨㄤˊ ㄍㄨㄥ | imperial palace |
| 14 | 故宮 | gùgōng | ㄍㄨˋ ㄍㄨㄥ | lit. Old Palace ; the Forbidden City |
| 15 | 現代 | xiàndài | ㄒㄧㄢˋ ㄉㄞˋ | contemporary; modern |
| 16 | 奇觀 | qíguān | ㄑㄧˊ ㄍㄨㄢ | marvel; wonder |
| 17 | 遊覽 | yóulǎn | ㄧㄡˊ ㄌㄢˇ | to travel |
| 18 | 四面八方 | sìmiànbāfāng | ㄙˋ ㄇㄧㄢˋ ㄅㄚ ㄈㄤ | all directions; far and near |
| 19 | 舉行 | jǔxíng | ㄐㄩˇ ㄒㄧㄥˊ | to hold (a ceremony) |
| 20 | 升旗 | shēngqí | ㄕㄥ ㄑㄧˊ | to raise the flag |
| 21 | 儀式 | yíshì | ㄧˊ ㄕˋ | ceremony |
| 22 | 等候 | děnghòu | ㄉㄥˇ ㄏㄡˋ | to wait |
| 23 | 觀看 | guānkàn | ㄍㄨㄢ ㄎㄢˋ | to watch |
| 24 | 下山 | xiàshān | ㄒㄧㄚˋ ㄕㄢ | to set (sun) |
| 25 | 一群一群 | yīqúnyīqún | ㄧ ㄑㄩㄣˊ ㄧ ㄑㄩㄣˊ | group after group |
| 26 | 降旗 | jiàngqí | ㄐㄧㄤˋ ㄑㄧˊ | the lowering of the flag |
| 27 | 國慶節 | guóqìngjié | ㄍㄨㄛˊ ㄑㄧㄥˋ ㄐㄧㄝˊ | National Day |
| 28 | 慶祝 | qìngzhù | ㄑㄧㄥˋ ㄓㄨˋ | to celebrate |
| 29 | 活動 | huódòng | ㄏㄨㄛˊ ㄉㄨㄥˋ | activity; performance |
| 30 | 國旗 | guóqí | ㄍㄨㄛˊ ㄑㄧˊ | national flag |
| 31 | 鮮花 | xiānhuā | ㄒㄧㄢ ㄏㄨㄚ | fresh flowers |
| 32 | 氣球 | qìqiú | ㄑㄧˋ ㄑㄧㄡˊ | balloon |
| 33 | 政府 | zhèngfǔ | ㄓㄥˋ ㄈㄨˇ | government |
| 34 | 從那以後 | cóngnàyǐhòu | ㄘㄨㄥˊ ㄋㄚˋ ㄧˇ ㄏㄡˋ | from then on |
| 35 | 元首 | yuánshǒu | ㄩㄢˊ ㄕㄡˇ | head of state |
| 36 | 人物 | rénwù | ㄖㄣˊ ㄨˋ | figure |

| | | | | |
|---|---|---|---|---|
| 37 | 人群 | rénqún | ㄖㄣˊ ㄑㄩㄣˊ | crowd |
| 38 | 講話 | jiǎnghuà | ㄐㄧㄤˇ ㄏㄨㄚˋ | to make a speech |
| 39 | 來賓 | láibīn | ㄌㄞˊ ㄅㄧㄣ | to visit |
| 40 | 壯觀 | zhuàngguān | ㄓㄨㄤˋ ㄍㄨㄢ | magnificent |
| 41 | 人民大會堂 | rénmín dàhuìtáng | ㄖㄣˊ ㄇㄧㄣˊ ㄉㄚˋ ㄏㄨㄟˋ ㄊㄤˊ | Great Hall of the People |
| 42 | 博物館 | bówùguǎn | ㄅㄛˊ ㄨˋ ㄍㄨㄢˇ | museum |
| 43 | 文物 | wénwù | ㄨㄣˊ ㄨˋ | historical relics |
| 44 | 大樓 | dàlóu | ㄉㄚˋ ㄌㄡˊ | building |
| 45 | 參觀 | cānguān | ㄘㄢ ㄍㄨㄢ | to visit; to go sightseeing |
| 46 | 放風箏 | fàngfēngzhēng | ㄈㄤˋ ㄈㄥ ㄓㄥ | to fly a kite |
| 47 | 幾米長 | jǐmǐcháng | ㄐㄧˇ ㄇㄧˇ ㄔㄤˊ | several meters long |
| 48 | 日子 | rìzi | ㄖˋ ㄗ˙ | day; date |
| 49 | 親眼 | qīnyǎn | ㄑㄧㄣ ㄧㄢˇ | with one's own eyes |
| 50 | 一般 | yībān | ㄧ ㄅㄢ | normal; ordinary |
| 51 | 四處 | sìchù | ㄙˋ ㄔㄨˋ | everywhere |
| 52 | 大街 | dàjiē | ㄉㄚˋ ㄐㄧㄝ | avenue |
| 53 | 長安街 | chángānjiē | ㄔㄤˊ ㄢ ㄐㄧㄝ | Avenue of Eternal Peace |
| 54 | 地下 | dìxià | ㄉㄧˋ ㄒㄧㄚˋ | underground |
| 55 | 鐵道 | tiědào | ㄊㄧㄝˇ ㄉㄠˋ | railway |
| 56 | 地鐵 | dìtiě | ㄉㄧˋ ㄊㄧㄝˇ | subway |
| 57 | 經過 | jīngguò | ㄐㄧㄥ ㄍㄨㄛˋ | to pass through |
| 58 | 正陽門 | Zhèngyángmén | ㄓㄥˋ ㄧㄤˊ ㄇㄣˊ | name of one of the old city gates |
| 59 | 環繞 | huánrào | ㄏㄨㄢˊ ㄖㄠˋ | encircle; surround |

| | | | | |
|---|---|---|---|---|
| 60 | 決定 | juédìng | ㄐㄩㄝˊ ㄉㄧㄥˋ | *to decide* |
| 61 | 物力 | wùlì | ㄨˋ ㄌㄧˋ | *material resources* |
| 62 | 大不一樣 | dàbùyīyàng | ㄉㄚˋ ㄅㄨˋ ㄧ ㄧㄤˋ | *very different* |
| 63 | 人口 | rénkǒu | ㄖㄣˊ ㄎㄡˇ | *population* |
| 64 | 天壇 | tiāntán | ㄊㄧㄢ ㄊㄢˊ | *Heavenly Temple* |
| 65 | 頤和園 | yíhéyuán | ㄧˊ ㄏㄜˊ ㄩㄢˊ | *Summer Palace* |

# 第一章　天安门

　　北京[1]是中国的首都[2]，天安门[3]是首都的象征[4]。当说到北京的时候，人们第一个想到的就是天安门，天安门原来是北京的一个地方的名字，也是一个门的名字，这个门很大很大，是古时候北京城的一个主要的城门[5]，那时候天安门就好像是皇帝[6]家的大门，站在天安门上可以看得很远很远。

　　天安门的前面有一条小河，是为了保护[7]皇帝的家。所以，这条河也叫护城河[8]，护城河上有一座桥[9]，叫作金水桥[10]。天安门的前面现在是一个很大很大的广场[11]，叫作天安门广场。天安门的后面是一座非常大的建筑群[12]，那是以前皇帝住的地方，因为那是古时候的皇宫[13]，所以中国人把它叫作"故宫[14]"。

　　天安门广场是世界上第二大的广场，是现代[15]中国的一大奇观[16]，它在今天中国人心里是一个非常重要的地方。每天都有许多人来这里游览[17]，他们从中国的四面八方[18]来，从世界的各个国家来。每天早晨，天安门广场上都会举行[19]升旗[20]的仪式[21]，天刚刚亮，太阳还没有升起来的时候，人们就等候[22]在这里观看[23]升旗仪式。太阳下山[24]的时候，游览的人们又一群一群[25]地等候在这里，观看降旗[26]仪式。

每年的十月，是中国的国庆节[27]，这个时候，在广场上会举行许多的庆祝[28]活动[29]，天安门广场非常地美丽。国旗[30]、红旗、各种颜色的鲜花[31]和节日的气球[32]到处都是。穿着漂亮衣服的人们，都会成群地来到这里一起庆祝。一九四九年的十月一号，中国政府[33]在这里举行了第一个国庆节，从那以后[34]，每年的这个时候，全中国的人民都一起举行庆祝活动，天安门就是这个节日的中心。

每一次国家重大的节日，政府都会在这里举行活动，国家元首[35]和政府重要的人物[36]都要在天安门的城门上，对天安门广场上的人群[37]和全中国人民讲话[38]。同时，天安门广场也是中国政府欢迎外国政府来宾[39]的地方，每一次外国元首来中国访问，中国政府都要在天安门广场上举行欢迎仪式和许多活动，欢迎他们到中国来。

广场的四面都有许多高大且壮观[40]的建筑物，广场的西面是人民大会堂[41]，这里是国家开大会的地方，每年有许多重要的大会都在这里举行。广场的东面是中国最大的历史博物馆[42]，里面可以看到许多介绍中国历史的文物[43]。在天安门广场的附近还有很多重要的政府大楼[44]，这些地方也是游览的人们常来参观[45]的地方。

因为天安门广场上非常大，所以经常有人来这里放风筝[46]，虽然在广场上可以买到各种好看的风筝，许多北京人还是喜欢自己做的风筝，他们的风筝有的是几米长[47]，还有的是十几米长，当然，他们的风筝是做得非常好的。除了冬天和政府有活动的日子[48]，差不多每天你都可以在这里看到放风筝。许多人来北京，也一定要到天安门广场来，亲眼[49]观看这个有趣的活动。

八十年代以前，天安门的城门是不让一般[50]的人上去的。在节日里，只有政府重要的人物和他们请的客人和朋友才能上去。他们在那里观看在广场上举行的庆祝活动。到了九十年代，政府才开放天安门，让人们四处[51]参观。从那以后，每天都有许多人到天安门城门上，参观这个古时候皇帝家的大门。到了天安门的上面，你就会明白，当时的皇帝为什么要建这么大的城门，你就会知道天安门广场有多大。

天安门和天安门广场的中间有一条大街[52]，叫作长安街[53]。你一定很奇怪，为什么这些名字里面都有一个"安"字，"安"在中文里就是平安的意思，中国人认为"安"

是一个非常有福的字。长安街是一条北京主要的大街，因为原来的长安街从东到西有十公里长，所以也叫做"十里长街"，长安街的下面是北京的地下[54]铁道[55]，也叫做地铁[56]，过去政府不让地铁从天安门下面经过[57]，到了九十年代，政府才让地铁从长安街下面经过。

天安门广场的南面是正阳门[58]，正阳门是一座古城门，五十年代以前正阳门还是原来的样子，在正阳门的两边是古城墙，古城墙的里面就是原来的北京。在古时候，正阳门的古城墙和天安门的古城墙之间住的是一般的老百姓，只有皇帝和皇帝的家人才能住在天安门的里面，正阳门两边的古城墙很长很长，环绕[59]着古时候的北京。这个古城墙一直到五十年代的时候还在。

从五十年代起，政府觉得古城墙里面的北京太小了，就决定[60]拿走古城墙，结果，政府花了很多的人力和物力[61]把古城墙拿走，并在古城墙的地方建了一条环绕北京的公路，并在这条公路的下面建了一条环绕北京的地铁。从那以后——特别是经过最近几十年的变化，北京的样子和以前大不一样[62]了，北京的人口[63]也比原来多了许多。

今天的北京已经比原来大多了，不再是原来古城墙里面的北京了。但是，许多的北京人还是认为古城墙里面的北京才是真正的北京。虽然，今天的北京与四十多年前的北京很不一样，政府还是希望保护古时候的建筑，所以政府规定在北京不可以建特别高的建筑。许多古时候的建筑，像故宫，天坛[64]和颐和园[65]政府都特别花人力和物力来保护。这些古建筑代表了中国的历史和文化，在天安门这个地方，你可以观看到中国的过去和现在；你也可以看见中国的将来。

## 阅读理解

1. 天安门广场有多大？
2. 每天在天安间广场有什么仪式？
3. 天安门广场为什么这么重要？
4. 广场前面的大街叫什么名字？
5. 为什么天安门的城门不让一般人上去？
6. 为什么政府要拿走北京的古城墙？
7. 为什么政府不让地铁从天安门的下面经过？

## 生字

| 1 | 北京 | běijīng | Beijing, the capitol of the People's Republic of China |
| 2 | 首都 | shǒudū | capitol |
| 3 | 天安门 | tiānānmén | The Gate of Heavenly Peace |
| 4 | 象征 | xiàngzhēng | symbol |
| 5 | 城门 | chéngmén | city gate |

| | | | |
|---|---|---|---|
| 6 | 皇帝 | huángdì | emperor |
| 7 | 保护 | bǎohù | to protect |
| 8 | 护城河 | hùchénghé | moat |
| 9 | 桥 | qiáo | bridge |
| 10 | 金水桥 | jīnshuǐqiáo | Golden Bridge |
| 11 | 广场 | guǎngchǎng | square |
| 12 | 建筑群 | jiànzhùqún | group of buildings |
| 13 | 皇宫 | huánggōng | imperial palace |
| 14 | 故宫 | gùgōng | lit. Old Palace; the Forbidden City |
| 15 | 现代 | xiàndài | contemporary; modern |
| 16 | 奇观 | qíguān | marvel; wonder |
| 17 | 游览 | yóulǎn | to travel |
| 18 | 四面八方 | sìmiànbāfāng | all directions; far and near |
| 19 | 举行 | jǔxíng | to hold (a ceremony) |
| 20 | 升旗 | shēngqí | to raise the flag |
| 21 | 仪式 | yíshì | ceremony |
| 22 | 等候 | děnghòu | to wait |
| 23 | 观看 | guānkàn | to watch |
| 24 | 下山 | xiàshān | to set (sun) |
| 25 | 一群一群 | yīqúnyīqún | group after group |
| 26 | 降旗 | jiàngqí | the lowering of the flag |
| 27 | 国庆节 | guóqìngjié | National Day |
| 28 | 庆祝 | qìngzhù | to celebrate |
| 29 | 活动 | huódòng | activity; performance |
| 30 | 国旗 | guóqí | national flag |
| 31 | 鲜花 | xiānhuā | fresh flowers |
| 32 | 气球 | qìqiú | balloon |
| 33 | 政府 | zhèngfǔ | government |
| 34 | 从那以后 | cóngnàyǐhòu | from then on |
| 35 | 元首 | yuánshǒu | head of state |
| 36 | 人物 | rénwù | figure |
| 37 | 人群 | rénqún | crowd |

| 38 | 讲话 | jiǎnghuà | to make a speech |
| 39 | 来宾 | láibīn | to visit |
| 40 | 壮观 | zhuàngguān | magnificent |
| 41 | 人民大会堂 | rénmíndàhuìtáng | Great Hall of the People |
| 42 | 博物馆 | bówùguǎn | museum |
| 43 | 文物 | wénwù | historical relics |
| 44 | 大楼 | dàlóu | building |
| 45 | 参观 | cānguān | to visit; to go sightseeing |
| 46 | 放风筝 | fàngfēngzhēng | to fly a kite |
| 47 | 几米长 | jǐmǐcháng | several meters long |
| 48 | 日子 | rìzi | day; date |
| 49 | 亲眼 | qīnyǎn | with one's own eyes |
| 50 | 一般 | yībān | normal; ordinary |
| 51 | 四处 | sìchù | everywhere |
| 52 | 大街 | dàjiē | avenue |
| 53 | 长安街 | chángānjiē | Avenue of Eternal Peace |
| 54 | 地下 | dìxià | underground |
| 55 | 铁道 | tiědào | railway |
| 56 | 地铁 | dìtiě | subway |
| 57 | 经过 | jīngguò | to pass through |
| 58 | 正阳门 | Zhèngyángmén | name of one of the old city gates |
| 59 | 环绕 | huánrào | encircle; surround |
| 60 | 决定 | juédìng | to decide |
| 61 | 物力 | wùlì | material resources |
| 62 | 大不一样 | dàbùyīyàng | very different |
| 63 | 人口 | rénkǒu | population |
| 64 | 天坛 | tiāntán | Heavenly Temple |
| 65 | 颐和园 | yíhéyuán | Summer Palace |

# Chapter 1   Tian An Men - The Gate of Heavenly Peace

Beijing is the capital of China. Tian An Men is the symbol of the capital. When people talk about Beijing, the first thing they think about is Tian An Men. Tian An Men is the name of an area in Beijing, it is also the name of a gate. That gate is very, very big, it is one of the main city gates of the ancient city of Beijing. In ancient times, Tian An Men seemed like a big door to the emperor's palace. When standing in Tian An Men, you can see great distances.

In front of Tian An Men is a small river. It once served to protect the emperor and is therefore called a moat. Above the moat is a bridge called the "Golden Bridge." In front of the Tian An Men Gate is an expansive square called the Tian An Men Square. Behind Tian An Men is a very large group of buildings. That is where the emperor used to live. Because the palace dates back to olden times, the Chinese call it "Old Palace" (Forbidden City).

Tian An Men Square is the second largest square in the world and China's most spectacular attraction. It holds a very special place in the hearts of the Chinese.  Everyday it is visited by many people from all parts of China and from many different countries. Early in the morning, a flag raising ceremony is held everyday in Tian An Men Square. When it is just beginning to get light and the sun hasn't yet risen, people arrive to watch the ceremony. At sunset, group after group of visitors come to see the lowering of the flag.

Chinese National Day takes place every year in October. On that day, many National Day celebrations are held in Tian An Men and the square looks very beautiful. Everywhere there are national flags, red flags, multi-colored flowers, and holiday balloons. People dressed in beautiful clothes come in groups to celebrate the National Day. On the first of October, 1949, the Chinese government held the first National Day celebration in Tian An Men. Since then, on that day, all the people of China celebrate the National Day together. Tian An Men is the actual center of the holiday.

Whenever there is an important holiday, the Chinese government holds celebrations in the square. The heads of state and other important government personalities all stand on top of the Tian An Men Gate facing the crowds in the square to make their speeches. Tian An Men Square is also the place where the Chinese government welcome foreign dignitaries who are visiting China. Every time a foreign head of state comes to China, the Chinese government holds a welcoming ceremony and other performances in Tian An Men Square.

Surrounding the four sides of Tian An Men Square are many imposing and magnificent buildings. On the west side is the Great Hall of the People. It is where the country's plenary sessions are held; many important meetings are held there every year. On the east side of the square is China's largest history museum. It contains many of China's historic relics. There are many other important government buildings around Tian An Men Square. It is also a place where the tourists go for sightseeing.

Because Tian An Men Square is so very big, it is often used for kite flying. Although beautiful kites can be bought in the square, the people of Beijing prefer to make their own. Some of their kites are several meters long, some are more than ten meters long. The handmade kites are very well-made. Except for in winter or when the government has organized celebrations, one can see kites flying practically everyday. Everyone who visits Beijing ought to go to Tian An Men Square to see the many interesting activities with his or her own eyes.

Before the 1980s, ordinary people were not allowed through Tian An Men Gate. On the holidays, only important government figures and their guests and friends were allowed in the Old Palace. From the top they could observe the National Day activities in the square. It was only in the '90s that the government started allowing people to visit Tian An Men. Nowadays, people climb up onto the city gate of Tian An Men everyday and look at the emperor's great gate. When you come to the front of Tian An Men you will comprehend why the emperor wanted to have such a big city gate built. You will see how big Tian An Men Square actually is.

Between Tian An Men Square and Tian An Men Gate is a very large street called the Avenue of Eternal Peace. You must be wondering why the word "安" appears in all these names. "安" means "peace" in Chinese. The Chinese people believe that the word "安" is filled with good fortune. The Avenue of Eternal Peace is one of Beijing's main streets. Because this avenue lies on an east-west axis and is ten kilometers long, it is also called "Ten Li Avenue." Below the Avenue of Eternal Peace is the underground railway, also called the subway. In the past, the government didn't permit the subway to pass underneath Tian An Men. It was only in the '90s that it was allowed to pass under Tian An Men.

On the south side of Tian An Men Square is the Zheng Yang Gate. Zheng Yang Gate is one of the old city gates. Up until the 1950s, Zheng Yang Gate still had its original appearance. On either side of the gate were the city walls, and inside the walls lay the old city of Beijing. In olden times, ordinary people lived inside the walls between Zheng Yang Gate and Tian An Men Gate. Only the emperor and his family lived inside Tian An Men. The city walls on either side of Zheng Yang Gate were very, very long and they surrounded the ancient city of Beijing. The city wall remained until the 1950s.

In the 1950s, the government decided that the city inside the ancient walls was too small and that the walls should be torn down. The government used a huge amount of manpower and material resources to tear it down. In its place, a road was built encircling Beijing. Later on, the subway under this road encircling Beijing was built as well. Since the 1950s, and especially in the latter 1990s, there have been many changes. The population of Beijing has also greatly increased.

The city of Beijing has grown a great deal. It no longer lies within the city walls. However, many people believe that the real Beijing lies within the old city walls. Even though the Beijing of today is very different from the old Beijing, the government still wants to protect the old architecture. The government recently decided not to allow very tall buildings to be built. The government is spending large amounts of manpower and material resources to protect ancient structures such as the Forbidden City, the Heavenly Temple, and the Summer Palace. These ancient buildings represent China's history and culture. In Tian An Men, one can see both the past and the present. One can also see China's future.

# 第二章　京劇

　　京劇[1]是一種古老的中國藝術[2]。京劇的"京"字,意思是皇帝住的地方。所以,京劇就是古時候皇宮裏的藝術,只有皇帝和他的家人才可以觀看這種藝術。那時候,每次節日來到了，皇帝就要在家裏看京劇，如果是特別重大的節日，皇帝就會在家裏看一個星期的京劇。

京劇裏其實有許多種的藝術，不同地方的演員又有不同的表演[3]風格[4]。京劇的表演包括[5] "唱[6]"、"念"、"坐"、"打"四個方面。"唱"就是歌唱[7]。在一場京劇裏，演員大部分的表演時間是在唱。所以，京劇有一點像西方的歌劇[8]。不過京劇和西方的歌劇有很大的不同。

表演的第二個方面是"念"。"念"就是說話或者對話。不過在京劇裏，演員的說話又不很像平常我們的說話，他們要用特別的方法來說話，不要說[9]外國人聽不懂京劇裏的說話，就是現在的中國人也很難聽懂。

同樣地，京劇演員"坐"的樣子也和平常人坐的樣子不一樣。"打"就是打仗的意思，這是因爲京劇裏經常有古代打仗[10]的故事，所以演員們需要表演古代打仗的樣子。一個京劇演員必須學會"唱"、"念"、"坐"、"打"這四種藝術，他必須[11]表演得特別好，才會讓觀看的人看懂，並且對京劇有興趣。

京劇表演的內容，主要是歷史上發生的事情。有皇帝特別愛護[12]人民的故事，也有的故事是關於[13]歷史上特別壞[14]的皇帝，不過，許多皇帝不喜歡看這樣的京劇故事。另外，有的京劇故事是講孩子是怎樣對他的爸爸和媽媽好。還有一些，是關於國王和他手下的人的故事。這些皇帝手下[15]的人非常好，對皇帝一直不變心[16]，皇帝最喜歡看這樣的京劇了。

現在，中國像許多國家一樣不再有皇帝了。這樣，一般老百姓[17]可以很容易看到京劇這種藝術了，過去幾十年來，京劇有了很大的發展[18]，在中國的各個地方，各大城市都有京劇劇院[19]。當然，中國最好的京劇劇院還是在北京，最好的京劇演員還是在北京，這是因為京劇和北京有非常大的關係[20]。古時候的"京"就是現在的北京，從前有許多的皇帝都住在北京。一百年來，各時候的中國政府也都把北京做為首都，因為這個原因，從古時候到現在，北京城裏住著許多的京劇藝術家。

北京人非常喜歡京劇，每天吃完了晚飯，人們就坐在院子裏休息。這時候大家就一起談起京劇來，有的人還學著唱京劇，學那些演員的表演和樣子，許多小孩子就是這樣從小跟著大人學，對京劇有了興趣，這些小孩子中間[21]，後來也有的人成了很有名的京劇演員。與[22]世界上其他的藝術來比[23]，京劇是一種非常特別的藝術。在北京，喜歡京劇的人不但常常會在一起談京劇，也會在一起表演他們喜歡的京劇。他們雖然不是演員，可是還是有很多人來看他們表演。

有一個地方常常可以看到京劇表演的，就是茶館[24]。以前，許多北京的茶館裏都有京劇的表演，茶館是北京人休息、談天[25]的地方，很像西方的咖啡店[26]。在北京有很多很多的茶館，每一個茶館裏，都有一個給人表演的地方，喜歡京劇的人就在這裏表演京劇。以前北京人一有時間，都要去茶館，坐下來喝一杯茶。他們一邊聽京劇，一邊與熟人和朋友談最近發生的事情。所以，茶館裏非常熱鬧[27]，演員唱京劇的聲音，茶館的客人喝茶和談話的聲音，都一直不停。有的時候，你都不知道人們是在聽京劇，還是在談話喝茶。人們有那麼多的話說，是因為茶館是那時候北京人社會生活中心，許多北京人都是在茶館裏知道每天發生的事情。

八十年代開始，中國開始向西方學習。因為中國的開放[28]和發展，生活開始有了很大的變化，而且變化越來越快。西方的現代音樂也開始在中國熱起來，為許多中國的年輕人歡迎和接受。喜歡京劇的年輕人越來越少。年輕人認為京劇的風格太慢，而且京劇裏表現的都是古時候的故事，他們覺得，京劇和他們的生活越來越沒有太大的關係。年級大的人卻覺得，京劇是中國文化裏重要的一部分[29]，看京劇可以學習到許多歷史和傳統的東西。可是年輕人覺得，歷史和傳統[30]在學校裏已經學了很多了，京劇雖然很好，但是年輕人更需要的是一些新的東西。

也有一些年輕人特別喜歡京劇，他們認為京劇是一門很好的藝術。京劇裏有許多好的東西，他們可以把這些東西表現在其它的藝術上，慢慢地，開始有一些人用京劇的音樂來唱現代歌[31]。年輕人特別喜歡這些現代歌，老年人卻覺得，這些現代歌不好，京劇不應該是這個樣子。後來，京劇的藝術家們就開始寫一些新的京劇，這些京劇都是關於現代的人和事，京劇開始有了現代的風格，現在，喜歡京劇的年輕人越來越多了。年輕的京劇演員也多起來了，在北京，有的小孩子才五、六歲，就會演唱京劇了。

　　因為現代生活的變化，北京的茶館越來越少了，可是北京人喜歡京劇的人還是很多，每天到了晚上，人們就帶著茶水[32]來到公園裏，他們隨便坐下，聽人唱起京劇來。這個時候，你差不多可以在每一個北京公園裏聽到唱京劇的聲音[33]，有人說京劇是北京人的藝術，看來[34]這是有道理的。

## 閱讀理解

一、京劇是什麼意思？
二、京劇的表演包括哪四個方面？
三、古時候京劇主要是給誰看的？
四、現代的京劇有什麼變化？
五、現代的年輕人為什麼不容易喜歡京劇？
六、你覺得京劇重要嗎？為什麼？
七、你聽過京劇嗎？談談你的印象。

## 生字

| | | | | |
|---|---|---|---|---|
| 1 | 京劇 | jīngjù | ㄐㄧㄥ ㄐㄩˋ | Beijing Opera |
| 2 | 藝術 | yìshù | ㄧˋ ㄕㄨˋ | art; art form |
| 3 | 表演 | biǎoyǎn | ㄅㄧㄠˇ ㄧㄢˇ | to perform; performance |
| 4 | 風格 | fēnggé | ㄈㄥ ㄍㄜˊ | style |
| 5 | 包括 | bāokuò | ㄅㄠ ㄎㄨㄛˋ | to include |
| 6 | 唱 | chàng | ㄔㄤˋ | to sing |
| 7 | 歌唱 | gēchàng | ㄍㄜ ㄔㄤˋ | to sing |
| 8 | 歌劇 | gējù | ㄍㄜ ㄐㄩˋ | opera |
| 9 | 不要說 | bùyàoshuō | ㄅㄨˋ ㄧㄠˋ ㄕㄨㄛ | not only |
| 10 | 打仗 | dǎzhàng | ㄉㄚˇ ㄓㄤˋ | to battle; war |
| 11 | 必須 | bìxū | ㄅㄧˋ ㄒㄩ | must |
| 12 | 愛護 | àihù | ㄞˋ ㄏㄨˋ | to cherish; to love |
| 13 | 關於 | guānyú | ㄍㄨㄢ ㄩˊ | about; concerned with |
| 14 | 壞 | huài | ㄏㄨㄞˋ | evil; bad |

| | | | | |
|---|---|---|---|---|
| 15 | 手下 | shǒuxià | ㄕㄡˇ ㄒㄧㄚˋ | vassal |
| 16 | 變心 | biànxīn | ㄅㄧㄢˋ ㄒㄧㄣ | to cease to be faithful |
| 17 | 老百姓 | lǎobǎixìng | ㄌㄠˇ ㄅㄞˇ ㄒㄧㄥˋ | lit. the Old Hundred Names; ordinary folk |
| 18 | 發展 | fāzhǎn | ㄈㄚ ㄓㄢˇ | to develop |
| 19 | 劇院 | jùyuàn | ㄐㄩˋ ㄩㄢˋ | the theatre; opera house |
| 20 | 關係 | guānxì | ㄍㄨㄢ ㄒㄧˋ | relationship |
| 21 | 中間 | zhōngjiān | ㄓㄨㄥ ㄐㄧㄢ | in the midst; among |
| 22 | 與 | yǔ | ㄩˇ | with; and |
| 23 | 來比 | láibǐ | ㄌㄞˊ ㄅㄧˇ | to compare |
| 24 | 茶館 | cháguǎn | ㄔㄚˊ ㄍㄨㄢˇ | tea house |
| 25 | 談天 | tántiān | ㄊㄢˊ ㄊㄧㄢ | to chat |
| 26 | 咖啡店 | kāfēidiàn | ㄎㄚ ㄈㄟ ㄉㄧㄢˋ | coffee shop |
| 27 | 熱鬧 | rènào | ㄖㄜˋ ㄋㄠˋ | lively; exciting |
| 28 | 開放 | kāifàng | ㄎㄞ ㄈㄤˋ | to open up |
| 29 | 一部分 | yībùfèn | ㄧ ㄅㄨˋ ㄈㄣˋ | one part of |
| 30 | 傳統 | chuántǒng | ㄔㄨㄢˊ ㄊㄨㄥˇ | tradition |
| 31 | 現代歌 | xiàndàigē | ㄒㄧㄢˋ ㄉㄞˋ ㄍㄜ | contemporary songs |
| 32 | 茶水 | cháshuǐ | ㄔㄚˊ ㄕㄨㄟˇ | tea |
| 33 | 聲音 | shēngyīn | ㄕㄥ ㄧㄣ | voice |
| 34 | 看來 | kànlái | ㄎㄢˋ ㄌㄞˊ | it seems |

# 第二章 京剧

京剧[1]是一种古老的中国艺术[2]。京剧的"京"字,意思是皇帝住的地方。所以,京剧就是古时候皇宫里的艺术,只有皇帝和他的家人才可以观看这种艺术。那时候,每次节日来到了,皇帝就要在家里看京剧,如果是特别重大的节日,皇帝就会在家里看一个星期的京剧。

京剧里其实有许多种的艺术,不同地方的演员又有不同的表演[3]风格[4]。京剧的表演包括[5]"唱[6]"、"念"、"坐"、"打"四个方面。"唱"就是歌唱[7]。在一场京剧里,演员大部分的表演时间是在唱。所以,京剧有一点像西方的歌剧[8]。不过京剧和西方的歌剧有很大的不同。

表演的第二个方面是"念"。"念"就是说话或者对话。不过在京剧里,演员的说话又不很像平常我们的说话,他们要用特别的方法来说话,不要说[9]外国人听不懂京剧里的说话,就是现在的中国人也很难听懂。

同样地，京剧演员"坐"的样子也和平常人坐的样子不一样。"打"就是打仗的意思，这是因为京剧里经常有古代打仗[10]的故事，所以演员们需要表演古代打仗的样子。一个京剧演员必须学会"唱"、"念"、"坐"、"打"这四种艺术，他必须[11]表演得特别好，才会让观看的人看懂，并且对京剧有兴趣。

京剧表演的内容，主要是历史上发生的事情。有皇帝特别爱护[12]人民的故事，也有的故事是关于[13]历史上特别坏[14]的皇帝，不过，许多皇帝不喜欢看这样的京剧故事。另外，有的京剧故事是讲孩子是怎样对他的爸爸和妈妈好。还有一些，是关于国王和他手下的人的故事。这些皇帝手下[15]的人非常好，对皇帝一直不变心[16]，皇帝最喜欢看这样的京剧了。

现在，中国像许多国家一样不再有皇帝了。这样，一般老百姓[17]可以很容易看到京剧这种艺术了，过去几十年来，京剧有了很大的发展[18]，在中国的各个地方，各大城市都有京剧剧院[19]。当然，中国最好的京剧剧院还是在北京，最好的京剧演员还是在北京，这是因为京剧和北京有非常大的关系[20]。古时候的"京"就是现在的北京，从前有许多的皇帝都住在北京。一百年来，各时候的中国政府也都把北京做为首都，因为这个原因，从古时候到现在，北京城里住着许多的京剧艺术家。

北京人非常喜欢京剧，每天吃完了晚饭，人们就坐在院子里休息。这时候大家就一起谈起京剧来，有的人还学着唱京剧，学那些演员的表演和样子，许多小孩子就是这样从小跟着大人学，对京剧有了兴趣，这些小孩子中间[21]，后来也有的人成了很有名的京剧演员。与[22]世界上其他的艺术来比[23]，京剧是一种非常特别的艺术。在北京，喜欢京剧的人不但常常会在一起谈京剧，也会在一起表演他们喜欢的京剧。他们虽然不是演员，可是还是有很多人来看他们表演。

有一个地方常常可以看到京剧表演的，就是茶馆[24]。以前，许多北京的茶馆里都有京剧的表演，茶馆是北京人休息、谈天[25]的地方，很像西方的咖啡店[26]。在北京有很多很多的茶馆，每一个茶馆里，都有一个给人表演的地方，喜欢京剧的人就在这里表演京剧。以前北京人一有时间，都要去茶馆，坐下来喝一杯茶。他们一边听京剧，一边与熟人和朋友谈最近发生的事情。所以，茶馆里非常热闹[27]，演员唱京剧的声音，茶馆的客人喝茶和谈话的声音，都一直不停。有的时候，你都不知道人们是在听京剧，还是在谈话喝茶。人们有那么多的话说，是因为茶馆是那时候北京人社会生活中心，许多北京人都是在茶馆里知道每天发生的事情。

八十年代开始，中国开始向西方学习。因为中国的开放[28]和发展，生活开始有了很大的变化，而且变化越来越快。西方的现代音乐也开始在中国热起来，为许多中国的年轻人欢迎和接受。喜欢京剧的年轻人越来越少。年轻人认为京剧的风格太慢，而且京剧里表现的都是古时候的故事，他们觉得，京剧和他们的生活越来越没有太大的关系。年级大的人却觉得，京剧是中国文化里重要的一部分[29]，看京剧可以学习到许多历史和传统的东西。可是年轻人觉得，历史和传统[30]在学校里已经学了很多了，京剧虽然很好，但是年轻人更需要的是一些新的东西。

也有一些年轻人特别喜欢京剧，他们认为京剧是一门很好的艺术。京剧里有许多好的东西，他们可以把这些东西表现在其它的艺术上，慢慢地，开始有一些人用京剧的音乐来唱现代歌[31]。年轻人特别喜欢这些现代歌，老年人却觉得，这些现代歌不好，京剧不应该是这个样子。后来，京剧的艺术家们就开始写一些新的京剧，这些京剧都是关于现代的人和事，京剧开始有了现代的风格，现在，喜欢京剧的年轻人越来越多了。年轻的京剧演员也多起来了，在北京，有的小孩子才五、六岁，就会演唱京剧了。

因为现代生活的变化，北京的茶馆越来越少了，可是北京人喜欢京剧的人还是很多，每天到了晚上，人们就带着茶水[32]来到公园里，他们随便坐下，听人唱起京剧来。

这个时候，你差不多可以在每一个北京公园里听到唱京剧的声音[33]，有人说京剧是北京人的艺术，看来[34]这是有道理的。

## 阅读理解

1. 京剧是什么意思？
2. 京剧的表演包括哪四个方面？
3. 古时候京剧主要是给谁看的？
4. 现代的京剧有什么变化？
5. 现代的年轻人为什么不容易喜欢京剧？
6. 你觉得京剧重要吗？为什么？
7. 你听过京剧吗？谈谈你的印象。

## 生字

| | | | |
|---|---|---|---|
| 1 | 京剧 | jīngjù | Beijing Opera |
| 2 | 艺术 | yìshù | art; art form |
| 3 | 表演 | biǎoyǎn | to perform; performance |
| 4 | 风格 | fēnggé | style |
| 5 | 包括 | bāokuò | to include |
| 6 | 唱 | chàng | to sing |
| 7 | 歌唱 | gēchàng | to sing |
| 8 | 歌剧 | gējù | opera |
| 9 | 不要说 | bùyàoshuō | not only |

| | | | |
|---|---|---|---|
| 10 | 打仗 | dǎzhàng | to battle; war |
| 11 | 必须 | bìxū | must |
| 12 | 爱护 | àihù | to cherish; to love |
| 13 | 关于 | guānyú | about; concerned with |
| 14 | 坏 | huài | evil; bad |
| 15 | 手下 | shǒuxià | vassal |
| 16 | 变心 | biànxīn | to cease to be faithful |
| 17 | 老百姓 | lǎobǎixìng | lit. the Old Hundred Names; ordinary folk |
| 18 | 发展 | fāzhǎn | to develop |
| 19 | 剧院 | jùyuàn | the theatre; opera house |
| 20 | 关系 | guānxì | relationship |
| 21 | 中间 | zhōngjiān | in the midst; among |
| 22 | 与 | yǔ | with; and |
| 23 | 来比 | láibǐ | to compare |
| 24 | 茶馆 | cháguǎn | tea house |
| 25 | 谈天 | tántiān | to chat |
| 26 | 咖啡店 | kāfēidiàn | coffee shop |
| 27 | 热闹 | rènào | lively; exciting |
| 28 | 开放 | kāifàng | to open up |
| 29 | 一部分 | yībùfèn | one part of |
| 30 | 传统 | chuántǒng | tradition |
| 31 | 现代歌 | xiàndàigē | contemporary songs |
| 32 | 茶水 | cháshuǐ | tea |
| 33 | 声音 | shēngyīn | voice |
| 34 | 看来 | kànlái | it seems |

# Chapter 2  Beijing Opera

Beijing Opera (Jing Ju) is one of China's ancient art forms. The word "Jing" (capital) signifies the place where the emperor lived. In former times, Beijing Opera was an art performed only inside the Imperial Palace. Only the emperor and his family were allowed to watch it. When there was a holiday, the emperor liked to stay indoors to enjoy an opera. If it was an especially important holiday, the emperor sometimes stayed and watched a whole week of Beijing Opera performances.

There are several art forms within the Beijing Opera, and actors from different parts of China also have different styles. The Beijing Opera contains four aspects: singing, speech, sitting, and fighting. Singing, of course, means singing songs. Within one piece, most of the actors' time is spent singing. That is why Beijing Opera resembles western opera. However, there are great differences between western and Beijing Opera.

The second aspect of a Beijing performance is speech. Speech means the actor speaks or is engaged in dialogue. However, Beijing Opera speech is not the same as everyday language. The actors speak in a particular fashion which means that not only foreigners don't understand it, but many Chinese have trouble understanding it as well.

Sitting refers to the manner in which the actors sit, which is also peculiar to Beijing Opera. Fighting refers to the act of war. Beijing Opera contains many stories of ancient wars and the actors must be able to portray ancient forms of battle. A Beijing Opera actor must be able to perform all four aspects of the art: singing, speech, sitting, and fighting. He must be able to act very well in order to make the audience understand and to arouse interest in the play.

The Beijing Opera mainly tells stories based on history. Some are stories about emperors who loved their people; some stories are about evil emperors. Most emperors would not have enjoyed that second kind of story, however. There were also stories that taught children how to behave towards their parents. Then there were those that told of a king and his vassals. These vassals were generally very loyal and never changed their attitudes toward their emperor. The last kind of story was the emperor's favorite.

Nowadays, China, like many other countries, no longer has an emperor and ordinary people can easily see Beijing Opera performances. Throughout the past decades, Beijing Opera has developed quite a bit. All the big cities in China now have their own opera house. Of course, the best Beijing Opera house is still in Beijing. The best Beijing Opera actors are also in Beijing because of the close relationship between Beijing Opera and Beijing. The word "Jing" (in Jing ju) refers to Beijing. Many emperors lived in Beijing, and Beijing has remained the capital during the last 100 years. That is why, since ancient times, many Beijing Opera performers have lived in Beijing.

The people of Beijing love the opera. After eating dinner, most people sit in the courtyard and relax. They sit together and talk about the opera. Some of them even learn how to sing parts of the opera and imitate one actor's performance and style. Many little children learn by copying the adults and they soon develop an interest. Later on, some of these children even turn into famous actors. Compared with other art forms in this world, Beijing Opera is truly special. Those who enjoy Beijing Opera not only sit and talk about it, but they also get together and perform the operas they like. Even though they are not professional actors, there is always an audience to watch them perform.

There is one place you will always be able to see opera being performed, and that is the teahouses. The teahouses were a place where people came to rest and chat, similar to western coffee shops. In Beijing, there were many teahouses. Each teahouse had a stage. Beijing Opera enthusiasts performed there. Whenever people had some free time, they used to come to the teahouse to have a cup of tea. They listened to Beijing Opera and chatted with their acquaintances or friends about the most recent news. The teahouses were very lively places. The voices of actors singing opera and the chatter of those drinking tea and talking never stopped. Sometimes you didn't know whether the people were really listening to the opera or whether they were just there to chat and drink tea. The reason why the people of Beijing often came to talk in teahouses was because they were the center of all social activities. Most Beijing residents got their daily news in the teahouses.

In the 1980s, China began to learn from the West. Because China opened to the West and started to develop, life changed a lot. The more it changed, the faster the changes came. For example, modern western music was introduced and welcomed by the Chinese youth. Fewer young people enjoyed listening to Beijing Opera. They thought the style was too slow and the stories told in the operas were about things in the distant past. They began to feel that their lives had very little to do with Beijing Opera. Older people still felt that Beijing Opera was an integral part of Chinese culture and that by studying it one could learn about history and tradition. The younger people, on the other hand, felt that they studied enough history and tradition in school. The younger generation needed something new.

There were a few young people fond of Beijing Opera who thought that Beijing Opera was a great art form. They felt that there were parts of opera that could be used to express things in a different art form. They borrowed the music from the Beijing Opera to sing contemporary songs. Many young people really enjoyed those songs. The elderly, however, didn't, and felt that Beijing Opera should not be sung this way. Later, some Beijing Opera performers started to write modern versions of Beijing Opera. Their subject matter concerned contemporary people and issues. Beijing Opera has taken on a new flavor and there are more and more young people who are listening to it. There are now more young Beijing Opera actors also. In Beijing, there are five and six-year-olds who can already perform Beijing Opera.

Because of the change of lifestyles, there are now fewer teahouses in Beijing. However, there are still many people who love the opera. Every evening, people bring their tea cups and go to the park. They sit and listen to the singers. In almost every park in Beijing, one can hear the sound of Beijing Opera. Some people say that opera is an art form belonging to the people of Beijing, it seems that there is truth in this.

# 第三章　北京大學

　　古時候，在中國這麼大的一個國家裏，只有四所大學，那時候，一般老百姓是不能上大學的，因爲沒有錢。這四所大學也不接受一般的學生，去大學念書的學生都是特別的好的學生，有的還是天才。這些學生畢業以後，他們大多數將來[2]都是做官[3]，也就是為皇帝服務的，所以，這四所大學就好像是皇家[4]大學一樣。

中國古代[5]的教育[6]其實[7]就是家庭[8]教育，中國歷史上的很多重要人物往往[9]是因為有很好的家庭教育，才使他們成為一個大人物[10]的。那時候，人們都是在家裏從小學習認識字，長大以後，父母就讓孩子們在家裏念書。條件好的家庭，父母就花錢[11]請一位老師，到家裏給孩子上課。

可是，古時候人們讀書是為了什麼呢？那時候，大多數[12]的中國人都是農民[13]，農民種田[14]很辛苦[15]，沒有時間[16]讀書，也不需要讀書。那時候的書都是告訴你怎麼做人[17]和做事[18]的，不是告訴你怎麼種田。所以，古時候人讀書是為了做大官的。

幾千年以後，中國發生了很大的變化。西方文化開始被介紹到中國社會。中國人開始接受很多西方的觀念[19]和事物[20]，比如：火車[21]、西藥[22]、和大學。西方的大學觀念和中國古時候的大學觀念有很大的不同，中國古時候的大學是為了少數人[23]，而西方的大學是為了更多的人得到教育。

北京大學就是這樣一個大學，它接受了西方的教育觀念，北京大學又叫做北大，它原來是皇帝辦[24]的學校。

一八九八年開始這所學校叫作北京大學。北大是當時中國最高的大學，也是中國最大和最好的大學，當時的北大就有二千多學生。

當時的北京大學，有很多有名的教授在那裏教書，這些教授都很熟悉西方的思想，他們都提出現代中國文化應該接受西方的觀念，向西方學習。從那時候開始，北京大學就成了中國新文化運動[25]的中心，一九一九年，中國有名的"五四"新文化運動[26]就是在北京大學開始的。

新文化運動提出要離開舊[27]的文化傳統和習慣[28]，去掉[29]中國社會裏無用[30]的觀念和思想。它提出中國人應該接受新的思想，比如科學和民主[31]的觀念。那時候的中國，已經不再有皇帝了，可是人們的思想還是很老舊，不喜歡接受新的東西，新文化運動還是給了當時[32]的中國社會很大的影響。

比如：那時候書上寫的古漢語[33]和一般老百姓日常[34]使用的語言不一樣，這樣，大多數的人就很難有了解[35]書上所說的學問[36]。所以，"五四"運動提出來，要政府在文章和書本[37]上使用大家日常所說、日常所用的漢語，也就是白話文[38]。這個白話文就是我們今天用的中文。白話文讓很多的中國人很容易地看書,並且得到知識[39]。有了白話文,讀書就變得容易多了。

所以,那時許多的新思想都是從北京大學提出來的,北大的許多教授或學生後來成爲[40]了中國非常有名的人。從那以後,北大成了一個提出新觀念、新思想的地方,很多時候,也是新的運動開始的地方,中國很多的年輕人都希望去北京大學讀書。

因爲北京大學有這樣好的歷史,各個時期[41]的中國政府都非常重視[42]北京大學。許多人從北京大學畢業後,都在政府裏做很重要的工作。在近幾十年裏,北京大學出了[43]許多的科學家,他們對現代中國社會有很大的影響。

現在的北京大學是在北京的西郊[44]。校園[45]的西面就是有名的皇帝花園-頤和園。校園的風景也是非常美麗,裏面有很多的綠樹、鮮花和很漂亮的人工湖[46]。北京大學現在有二萬多位學生在那裏學習。每年有幾千位從世界上各個國家來的留學生。從北大建校[47]以來,它一直被認爲是中國最好的大學。這裏有中國最好的教授和中國最好的學生。如果你到了北京沒有去北大遊覽,這會是一件很可惜[48]的事情。

## 閱讀理解

一、古時候中國人讀書是爲了什麼？
二、古代中國人是怎樣得到教育的？
三、什麼是"五四"新文化運動？
四、新文化運動是要接受什麼樣的新觀念？
五、漢語的變化對中國現代教育有什麼影響？
六、爲什麼說北京大學是新思想的中心？

## 生字

| | | | | |
|---|---|---|---|---|
| 1 | 接受 | jiēshòu | ㄐㄧㄝ ㄕㄡˋ | to accept |
| 2 | 將來 | jiānglái | ㄐㄧㄤ ㄌㄞˊ | the future |
| 3 | 做官 | zuòguān | ㄗㄨㄛˋ ㄍㄨㄢ | to secure an official position |
| 4 | 皇家 | huángjiā | ㄏㄨㄤˊ ㄐㄧㄚ | the imperial household |
| 5 | 古代 | gǔdài | ㄍㄨˇ ㄉㄞˋ | ancient times |
| 6 | 教育 | jiàoyù | ㄐㄧㄠˋ ㄩˋ | education |
| 7 | 其實 | qíshí | ㄑㄧˊ ㄕˊ | actually; in fact |
| 8 | 家庭 | jiātíng | ㄐㄧㄚ ㄊㄧㄥˊ | family; household |
| 9 | 往往 | wǎngwǎng | ㄨㄤˇ ㄨㄤˇ | frequently; often |
| 10 | 大人物 | dàrénwù | ㄉㄚˋ ㄖㄣˊ ㄨˋ | important person |
| 11 | 花錢 | huāqián | ㄏㄨㄚ ㄑㄧㄢˊ | to spend money |
| 12 | 大多數 | dàduōshù | ㄉㄚˋ ㄉㄨㄛ ㄕㄨˋ | the great majority |
| 13 | 農民 | nóngmín | ㄋㄨㄥˊ ㄇㄧㄣˊ | peasant |
| 14 | 種田 | zhòngtián | ㄓㄨㄥˋ ㄊㄧㄢˊ | to till the land |

## Life in Beijing

| | | | | |
|---|---|---|---|---|
| 15 | 辛苦 | xīnkǔ | ㄒㄧㄣ ㄎㄨˇ | hardship; tough |
| 16 | 時間 | shíjiān | ㄕˊ ㄐㄧㄢ | time |
| 17 | 做人 | zuòrén | ㄗㄨㄛˋ ㄖㄣˊ | human behavior |
| 18 | 做事 | zuòshì | ㄗㄨㄛˋ ㄕˋ | to handle one's affairs |
| 19 | 觀念 | guānniàn | ㄍㄨㄢ ㄋㄧㄢˋ | concept; idea |
| 20 | 事物 | shìwù | ㄕˋ ㄨˋ | object; thing |
| 21 | 火車 | huǒchē | ㄏㄨㄛˇ ㄔㄜ | train |
| 22 | 西藥 | xīyào | ㄒㄧ ㄧㄠˋ | western medicine |
| 23 | 少數人 | shǎoshùrén | ㄕㄠˇ ㄕㄨˋ ㄖㄣˊ | a small number of people; a minority |
| 24 | 辦 | bàn | ㄅㄢˋ | to handle; to manage; to run; to organize |
| 25 | 運動 | yùndòng | ㄩㄣˋ ㄉㄨㄥˋ | political movement |
| 26 | 五四新文化運動 | wǔsìxīnwén huàyùndòng | ㄨˇ ㄙˋ ㄒㄧㄣ ㄨㄣˊ ㄏㄨㄚˋ ㄩㄣˋ ㄉㄨㄥˋ | May Fourth New Culture Movement |
| 27 | 舊 | jiù | ㄐㄧㄡˋ | old |
| 28 | 習慣 | xíguàn | ㄒㄧˊ ㄍㄨㄢˋ | customs |
| 29 | 去掉 | qùdiào | ㄑㄩˋ ㄉㄧㄠˋ | to get rid of |
| 30 | 無用 | wúyòng | ㄨˊ ㄩㄥˋ | of no use |
| 31 | 民主 | mínzhǔ | ㄇㄧㄣˊ ㄓㄨˇ | democracy |
| 32 | 當時 | dāngshí | ㄉㄤ ㄕˊ | at that time |
| 33 | 古漢語 | gǔhànyǔ | ㄍㄨˇ ㄏㄢˋ ㄩˇ | classical Chinese |
| 34 | 日常 | rìcháng | ㄖˋ ㄔㄤˊ | daily |
| 35 | 了解 | liǎojiě | ㄌㄧㄠˇ ㄐㄧㄝˇ | to understand |
| 36 | 學問 | xuéwèn | ㄒㄩㄝˊ ㄨㄣˋ | knowledge; learning |
| 37 | 書本 | shūběn | ㄕㄨ ㄅㄣˇ | book |

| | | | | |
|---|---|---|---|---|
| 38 | 白話文 | báihuàwén | ㄅㄞˊ ㄏㄨㄚˋ ㄨㄣˊ | the vernacular |
| 39 | 知識 | zhīshí | ㄓ ㄕˊ | knowledge |
| 40 | 成為 | chéngwéi | ㄔㄥˊ ㄨㄟˊ | to turn into; to become |
| 41 | 時期 | shíqí | ㄕˊ ㄑㄧˊ | time period |
| 42 | 重視 | zhòngshì | ㄓㄨㄥˋ ㄕˋ | to attach importance to |
| 43 | 出了 | chūle | ㄔㄨ ㄌㄜ˙ | to come out of |
| 44 | 西郊 | xījiāo | ㄒㄧ ㄐㄧㄠ | in the west |
| 45 | 校園 | xiàoyuán | ㄒㄧㄠˋ ㄩㄢˊ | campus |
| 46 | 人工湖 | réngōnghú | ㄖㄣˊ ㄍㄨㄥ ㄏㄨˊ | artificial lake |
| 47 | 建校 | jiànxiào | ㄐㄧㄢˋ ㄒㄧㄠˋ | establishment of the school |
| 48 | 可惜 | kěxī | ㄎㄜˇ ㄒㄧ | a pity |

# 第三章　北京大学

古时候,在中国这么大的一个国家里,只有四所大学,那时候,一般老百姓是不能上大学的,因为没有钱。这四所大学也不接受[1]一般的学生,去大学念书的学生都是特别的好的学生,有的还是天才。这些学生毕业以后,他们大多数将来[2]都是做官[3],也就是为皇帝服务的,所以,这四所大学就好像是皇家[4]大学一样。

中国古代[5]的教育[6]其实[7]就是家庭[8]教育,中国历史上的很多重要人物往往[9]是因为有很好的家庭教育,才使他们成为一个大人物[10]的。那时候,人们都是在家里从小学习认识字,长大以后,父母就让孩子们在家里念书。条件好的家庭,父母就花钱[11]请一位老师,到家里给孩子上课。

可是,古时候人们读书是为了什么呢?那时候,大多数[12]的中国人都是农民[13],农民种田[14]很辛苦[15],没有时间[16]读书，也不需要读书。那时候的书都是告诉你怎么做人[17]和做事[18]的，不是告诉你怎么种田。所以，古时候人读书是为了做大官的。

几千年以后，中国发生了很大的变化。西方文化开始被介绍到中国社会。中国人开始接受很多西方的观念[19]和事物[20]，比如：火车[21]、西药[22]、和大学。西方的大学观念和中国古时候的大学观念有很大的不同，中国古时候的大学是为了少数人[23]，而西方的大学是为了更多的人得到教育。

北京大学就是这样一个大学，它接受了西方的教育观念，北京大学又叫做北大，它原来是皇帝办[24]的学校。一八九八年开始这所学校叫作北京大学。北大是当时中国最高的大学，也是中国最大和最好的大学，当时的北大就有二千多学生。

当时的北京大学，有很多有名的教授在那里教书，这些教授都很熟悉西方的思想，他们都提出现代中国文化应该接受西方的观念，向西方学习。从那时候开始，北京大学就成了中国新文化运动[25]的中心，一九一九年，中国有名的"五四"新文化运动[26]就是在北京大学开始的。

新文化运动提出要离开旧[27]的文化传统和习惯[28]，去掉[29]中国社会里无用[30]的观念和思想。它提出中国人应该接受新的思想，比如科学和民主[31]的观念。那时候的中国，已经不再有皇帝了，可是人们的思想还是很老旧，不喜欢接受新的东西，新文化运动还是给了当时[32]的中国社会很大的影响。

比如：那时候书上写的古汉语[33]和一般老百姓日常[34]使用的语言不一样，这样，大多数的人就很难有了解[35]书上所说的学问[36]。所以，"五四"运动提出来，要政府在文章和书本[37]上使用大家日常所说、日常所用的汉语，也就是白话文[38]。这个白话文就是我们今天用的中文。白话文让很多的中国人很容易地看书，并且得到知识[39]。有了白话文，读书就变得容易多了。

所以，那时许多的新思想都是从北京大学提出来的，北大的许多教授或学生后来成为[40]了中国非常有名的人。从那以后，北大成了一个提出新观念、新思想的地方，很多时候，也是新的运动开始的地方，中国很多的年轻人都希望去北京大学读书。

因为北京大学有这样好的历史，各个时期[41]的中国政府都非常重视[42]北京大学。许多人从北京大学毕业后，都在政府里做很重要的工作。在近几十年里，北京大学出了[43]许多的科学家,他们对现代中国社会有很大的影响。

现在的北京大学是在北京的西郊[44]。校园[45]的西面就是有名的皇帝花园-颐和园。校园的风景也是非常美丽,里面有很多的绿树、鲜花和很漂亮的人工湖[46]。北京大学现在有二万多位学生在那里学习。每年有几千位从世界上各个国家来的留学生。从北大建校[47]以来,它一直被认为是中国最好的大学。这里有中国最好的教授和中国最好的学生。如果你到了北京没有去北大游览,这会是一件很可惜[48]的事情。

## 阅读理解

1. 古时候中国人读书是为了什么?
2. 古代中国人是怎样得到教育的?
3. 什么是"五四"新文化运动?
4. 新文化运动是要接受什么样的新观念?
5. 汉语的变化对中国现代教育有什么影响?
6. 为什么说北京大学是新思想的中心?

## 生字

| | | | |
|---|---|---|---|
| 1 | 接受 | jiēshòu | to accept |
| 2 | 将来 | jiānglái | the future |
| 3 | 做官 | zuòguān | to secure an official position |
| 4 | 皇家 | huángjiā | the imperial household |
| 5 | 古代 | gǔdài | ancient times |
| 6 | 教育 | jiàoyù | education |
| 7 | 其实 | qíshí | actually; in fact |
| 8 | 家庭 | jiātíng | family; household |
| 9 | 往往 | wǎngwǎng | frequently; often |
| 10 | 大人物 | dàrénwù | important person |
| 11 | 花钱 | huāqián | to spend money |
| 12 | 大多数 | dàduōshù | the great majority |
| 13 | 农民 | nóngmín | peasant |
| 14 | 种田 | zhòngtián | to till the land |
| 15 | 辛苦 | xīnkǔ | hardship; tough |
| 16 | 时间 | shíjiān | time |
| 17 | 做人 | zuòrén | human behavior |
| 18 | 做事 | zuòshì | to handle one's affairs |
| 19 | 观念 | guānniàn | concept; idea |
| 20 | 事物 | shìwù | object; thing |
| 21 | 火车 | huǒchē | train |
| 22 | 西药 | xīyào | western medicine |
| 23 | 少数人 | shǎoshùrén | a small number of people; a minority |
| 24 | 办 | bàn | to handle; to manage; to run; to organize |
| 25 | 运动 | yùndòng | political movement |

| | | | |
|---|---|---|---|
| 26 | 五四新文化运动 | wǔsìxīnwénhuà yùndòng | *May Fourth New Culture Movement* |
| 27 | 旧 | jiù | *old* |
| 28 | 习惯 | xíguàn | *customs* |
| 29 | 去掉 | qùdiào | *to get rid of* |
| 30 | 无用 | wúyòng | *of no use* |
| 31 | 民主 | mínzhǔ | *democracy* |
| 32 | 当时 | dāngshí | *at that time* |
| 33 | 古汉语 | gǔhànyǔ | *classical Chinese* |
| 34 | 日常 | rìcháng | *daily* |
| 35 | 了解 | liǎojiě | *to understand* |
| 36 | 学问 | xuéwèn | *knowledge; learning* |
| 37 | 书本 | shūběn | *book* |
| 38 | 白话文 | báihuàwén | *the vernacular* |
| 39 | 知识 | zhīshí | *knowledge* |
| 40 | 成为 | chéngwéi | *to turn into; to become* |
| 41 | 时期 | shíqí | *time period* |
| 42 | 重视 | zhòngshì | *to attach importance to* |
| 43 | 出了 | chūle | *to come out of* |
| 44 | 西郊 | xījiāo | *in the west* |
| 45 | 校园 | xiàoyuán | *campus* |
| 46 | 人工湖 | réngōnghú | *artificial lake* |
| 47 | 建校 | jiànxiào | *establishment of the school* |
| 48 | 可惜 | kěxī | *a pity* |

# Chapter 3  The University of Beijing

In ancient times, in spite of China's vast size, there were only four universities in the whole country. In those days, ordinary people could not go to a university because they had no money. What is more, those four universities didn't accept just any student. Those who went to universities to study were all exceptional students, some were geniuses. After graduating, the students generally ended up securing official positions. It seemed as if the universities were really imperial universities.

In ancient China, education meant being taught in one's own home. Often, many of China's historical personalities became important people because they received good education in their homes. In those days, children started learning how to write at home. Later on, when they were growing up, their parents made them study at home. If the conditions were favorable, parents paid for a teacher to come to their house to teach the children.

But why did people need to study in ancient times? The majority of the Chinese were peasants in those days and tilling the land was hard labor. People had no time to read and didn't need to study books. Books were about human behavior and how to handle one's affairs, not about farm work.  People who studied did so because they wanted to secure an official post.

Several thousand years later a great change came over China. Western culture began to be introduced into Chinese society. Chinese people were flooded with western ideas and western things such as trains, western medicine, and western universities. The western concept of higher education and the Chinese concept of universities were not the same. The old Chinese universities taught only a small group of people; western universities believed in bringing higher education to more people.

Beijing University is one of the universities that absorbed the western attitude toward education. Beijing University, which is also called "Bei Da," was a school initially run by the emperor. In 1898, the school was renamed Beijing University. At that time, Bei Da was the topmost university in China, it was also the largest. More than 2,000 students were enrolled in those days.

Many famous professors taught at Beijing University. These professors were familiar with western thought. They suggested that modern Chinese culture needed to accept western ideas and learn from the western world. Beijing University became the center of China's new cultural movement. The famous May 4th New Culture Movement of 1919 originated at Beijing University.

The New Culture Movement proposed leaving behind the old cultural traditions and habits and getting rid of concepts and theories that were of no use to modern Chinese society. The movement encouraged the Chinese to accept new ways of thinking such as science and democracy. At the time of the movement, China no longer had an emperor, but the people still had an old-fashioned way of thinking and didn't like accepting new ideas. In spite of that, the New Culture Movement greatly influenced Chinese society at the time.

One example of the movement's influence was seen in the language. Literary classical Chinese was very different from the Chinese spoken by ordinary people, which made it very difficult for most people to understand the meaning of books. During the May 4th Movement, it was proposed that the government use only modern Chinese or vernacular Chinese in articles and books. Vernacular Chinese is the Chinese we use today. Using the vernacular made reading books and obtaining knowledge easier for many Chinese. After the vernacular was introduced, studying became much easier.

In those days, many new ideologies originated at Beijing University. Many of the Bei Da professors and students later became famous personalities. Since that time, Bei Da has been a place where new ways of thinking and new ideologies are conceived. Very often it is also the place where new movements begin. Many young people dream of studying at Beijing University.

Because the history of Beijing University has been so exceptional, the government has placed a great deal of importance upon it. There are many Beijing University graduates who have accomplished great things in the government. During the most recent decades, many scientists have come out of Beijing University. Their influence on modern Chinese society has been tremendous.

Beijing University is now located in the west of the city. The famous imperial garden called the Summer Palace lies on the west side of the campus. The campus landscape is very picturesque, with many green trees, brightly colored flowers, and beautiful artificial lakes. There are now more than 20,000 students studying at Beijing University. There are also several thousand foreign students from different countries. Ever since it was established, Bei Da has been considered the best university in China. The best professors in China and the best students in China are all there. It would be a great pity if you go to Beijing but do not visit Bei Da.

# 第四章　故宮

　　故宮是以前皇帝在北京住的地方，意思就是皇宮。因為在過去的幾百年裏，許多皇帝都把北京定為首都，所以，皇宮就建在北京，這個皇宮就是今天的故宮。從天安門高大的城門走進去，你就到了故宮了，不過從天安門到皇帝真正住的地方，你還要走一些時候，經過許多高大的門。

故宮是一個非常大的建築群，這個建築群被圍在一個很大的院子裏，院子的牆非常高，院子裏面有九百九十九個房間，這也許是因為中國的皇帝都喜歡"九"這個數字。故宮裏面有許多房子，有的房子是給一般的人住，這些人都是每天為皇帝做事情的人，還有的房子是給保護皇帝的士兵[1]住的。

　　皇帝的太太叫做皇后[2]，皇后和孩子們都有自己的房子和院子。皇帝的院子很大，裏面有許多特別大的房子，皇帝就在這些地方開會，會見各種重要的人物和處理[3]國家每天的大事。

　　雖然故宮非常大，院子和房子都很多，可是皇帝卻並不喜歡老是住在這裏面，他喜歡在別的地方也建一些房子和院子。這樣，皇帝有的時候可以住在這裏，有的時候可以住在那裏，這些房子和院子不在北京城裏，而在北京附近的一些地方，這些地方都有山有水，風景十分美麗，夏天天氣很熱的時候，皇帝就去這些地方住，比如：北京的頤和園就是這樣的一個地方。

　　雖然皇帝住的地方很舒服[4]，但他還是想知道一般老百姓的生活是什麼樣子，他們每天吃什麼，他們住的地方怎麼樣，他們在想什麼。他希望他能有機會訪問他國家的人民[5]，但是，皇帝出去的時候，常常有許多人跟在他的左右前後[6]。如果人們知道他是皇帝，就不會把真正想要說的話告訴他了，古時候，人民是很怕皇帝的。

所以，皇帝就經常自己一個人出去，或者就帶一、兩個手下的人，他們穿上老百姓的簡單衣服，讓自己看起來像一般老百姓的樣子。他們不告訴家裏人他們要到哪裏去，也不告訴別人他們是誰，然後，皇帝就去訪問[7]北京城裏的老百姓。有時，他還在平民[8]的家裏吃飯，皇帝也很喜歡自己一個人去茶館，和北京的老百姓一起談天。

因為故宮每天晚上都要關門[9]，晚上到了一定的時間大門就關了，沒有人可以隨便進出[10]，皇帝因為不想讓別人們知道他出去的事情，所以時間一到，他就必須馬上回去。皇帝訪問老百姓的事情，最後還是讓人知道了，人民都很感謝[11]皇帝這樣來訪問他們，在中國歷史上，有不少這樣有趣[12]的故事。

古時候，如果有人來訪，要想見皇帝，他先要在一個大門外等候，那個大門叫做"午門[13]"。皇帝的士兵這時會跑進去報告[14]，皇帝同意了，來訪的客人才可以和皇帝見面。客人要跟著士兵，走過幾個門，然後才能最後見到皇帝。大概，每一個國家的皇帝都一樣，這些皇帝都怕來的客人會殺掉[15]皇帝自己。

古代的中國，皇帝在國家裏是最大的，皇帝要什麼就有什麼，想做什麼事就可以做什麼事，皇帝說的話，人民是不可以不聽的。所以，在中國歷史上，皇帝是一個影響國家和人民生活最重要的人。

中國歷史上的第一個皇帝叫"秦始皇[16]"，那時候，中國不是一個國家，而是七個國家，這七個小國之中，其中有一個叫秦國[17]，秦國的國王很有能力，他的國家雖然小，卻統一[18]了當時的整個[19]中國，這在中國歷史上是一件很大的事情。

秦國的國王統一了中國後，就不再叫自己是國王了，他叫自己是皇帝，意思就是國王的國王。因為中國古代的皇帝是從他開始的，所以歷史上我們又叫他"秦始皇"，他當了皇帝以後，做了很多歷史的大事，還建了非常有名的長城。據說[20]，他的皇宮在當時也很大，比現在的故宮還要大很多，可是，秦始皇也做了很多壞事[21]。比如：他不想讓人民知道歷史，他就燒[22]了全國[23]所有的書，還殺了成千上萬[24]的讀書人，所以，人民非常恨[25]這個皇帝。秦始皇死了以後，人們還是很恨他，就把他的皇宮燒了，據說這場[26]大火燒了好幾天[27]呢！

古時候在中國，每一個皇帝都是從年輕做到年老，死了以後，又讓自己的兒子做皇帝，兒子死了以後，兒子的兒子又繼續做皇帝。歷史上有很多皇帝對人民非常壞，他們不給國家平安，也不給人民幸福，這時，就有人起來把皇帝殺了。殺皇帝的人後來就自己做了皇帝，中國的歷史已經有幾千年了，其中換[28]了許許多多的皇帝，每一個皇帝都有自己的皇宮，中國的最後一個皇帝也有自己的皇宮，這個皇宮就是現在的故宮。

一九一一年以後，中國就不再有皇帝了。從那以後，故宮就變成了一個博物院[29]，讓人們來參觀中國古時候的歷史、文化、和建築風格。因為歷史上許多皇帝都把北京作為首都，所以在故宮裏面就有很多很貴重[30]和稀有[31]的文物，這些文物代表保留著古代的中國文化。現在，每天都有從世界各地來的人們遊覽參觀故宮，故宮成了古代中國歷史和文化的一個奇觀。

## 閱讀理解

一、故宮在什麼地方？
二、故宮裏面是什麼樣子？
三、為什麼古時候的人民怕皇帝？
四、皇帝為什麼要自己一個人出去訪問人民？
五、中國的第一個皇帝是誰？他做了什麼事？
六、古時候誰可以做皇帝？

七、從什麼時候開始，中國就沒有皇帝了？爲什麼？

八、古代中國換了多少朝代？多少皇帝？

九、談談你對電影"末代皇帝"的感想。

十、沒有皇帝以後，中國文化有哪些變化？

# 生字

| | | | | |
|---|---|---|---|---|
| 1 | 士兵 | shìbīng | ㄕˋ ㄅㄧㄥ | guard |
| 2 | 皇后 | huánghòu | ㄏㄨㄤˊ ㄏㄡˋ | empress |
| 3 | 處理 | chǔlǐ | ㄔㄨˇ ㄌㄧˇ | to handle |
| 4 | 舒服 | shūfú | ㄕㄨ ㄈㄨˊ | comfortable |
| 5 | 人民 | rénmín | ㄖㄣˊ ㄇㄧㄣˊ | the people |
| 6 | 左右前後 | zuǒyòu qiánhòu | ㄗㄨㄛˇ ㄧㄡˋ ㄑㄧㄢˊ ㄏㄡˋ | to be surrounded on all sides. |
| 7 | 訪問 | fǎngwèn | ㄈㄤˇ ㄨㄣˋ | to interview |
| 8 | 平民 | píngmín | ㄆㄧㄥˊ ㄇㄧㄣˊ | common |
| 9 | 關門 | guānmén | ㄍㄨㄢ ㄇㄣˊ | to lock or close the door |
| 10 | 進出 | jìnchū | ㄐㄧㄣˋ ㄔㄨ | to go in and out |
| 11 | 感謝 | gǎnxiè | ㄍㄢˇ ㄒㄧㄝˋ | to be grateful; to thank |
| 12 | 有趣 | yǒuqù | ㄧㄡˇ ㄑㄩˋ | interesting |
| 13 | 午門 | wǔmén | ㄨˇ ㄇㄣˊ | the gate where visitors waited until they were admitted to the emperor |
| 14 | 報告 | bàogào | ㄅㄠˋ ㄍㄠˋ | to report |
| 15 | 殺掉 | shādiào | ㄕㄚ ㄉㄧㄠˋ | to murder; to kill |

| | | | | |
|---|---|---|---|---|
| 16 | 秦始皇 | qínshǐhuáng | ㄑㄧㄣˊ ㄕˇ ㄏㄨㄤˊ | Qin Shi Huang, the first emperor of China |
| 17 | 秦國 | qínguó | ㄑㄧㄣˊ ㄍㄨㄛˊ | the Kingdom of Qin |
| 18 | 統一 | tǒngyī | ㄊㄨㄥˇ ㄧ | to unite |
| 19 | 整個 | zhěnggè | ㄓㄥˇ ㄍㄜ˙ | whole; entire |
| 20 | 據說 | jùshuō | ㄐㄩˋ ㄕㄨㄛ | legend |
| 21 | 壞事 | huàishì | ㄏㄨㄞˋ ㄕˋ | evil deeds |
| 22 | 燒 | shāo | ㄕㄠ | to burn |
| 23 | 全國 | quánguó | ㄑㄩㄢˊ ㄍㄨㄛˊ | the whole country |
| 24 | 成千上萬 | chéngqiānshàngwàn | ㄔㄥˊ ㄑㄧㄢ ㄕㄤˋ ㄨㄢˋ | tens of thousands |
| 25 | 恨 | hèn | ㄏㄣˋ | to hate |
| 26 | 這場 | zhècháng | ㄓㄜˋ ㄔㄤˊ | measure word; this |
| 27 | 好幾天 | hǎojǐtiān | ㄏㄠˇ ㄐㄧˇ ㄊㄧㄢ | many days |
| 28 | 換 | huàn | ㄏㄨㄢˋ | to change |
| 29 | 博物院 | bówùyuàn | ㄅㄛˊ ㄨˋ ㄩㄢˋ | museum (institute) |
| 30 | 貴重 | guìzhòng | ㄍㄨㄟˋ ㄓㄨㄥˋ | precious |
| 31 | 稀有 | xīyǒu | ㄒㄧ ㄧㄡˇ | rare |

# 第四章 故宫

　　故宫是以前皇帝在北京住的地方，意思就是皇宫。因为在过去的几百年里，许多皇帝都把北京定为首都，所以，皇宫就建在北京，这个皇宫就是今天的故宫。从天安门高大的城门走进去，你就到了故宫了，不过从天安门到皇帝真正住的地方，你还要走一些时候，经过许多高大的门。

　　故宫是一个非常大的建筑群，这个建筑群被围在一个很大的院子里，院子的墙非常高，院子里面有九百九十九个房间，这也许是因为中国的皇帝都喜欢"九"这个数字。故宫里面有许多房子，有的房子是给一般的人住，这些人都是每天为皇帝做事情的人，还有的房子是给保护皇帝的士兵[1]住的。

　　皇帝的太太叫做皇后[2]，皇后和孩子们都有自己的房子和院子。皇帝的院子很大，里面有许多特别大的房子，皇帝就在这些地方开会，会见各种重要的人物和处理[3]国家每天的大事。

虽然故宫非常大，院子和房子都很多，可是皇帝却并不喜欢老是住在这里面，他喜欢在别的地方也建一些房子和院子。这样，皇帝有的时候可以住在这里，有的时候可以住在那里，这些房子和院子不在北京城里，而在北京附近的一些地方，这些地方都有山有水，风景十分美丽，夏天天气很热的时候，皇帝就去这些地方住，比如：北京的颐和园就是这样的一个地方。

虽然皇帝住的地方很舒服[4]，但他还是想知道一般老百姓的生活是什么样子，他们每天吃什么，他们住的地方怎么样，他们在想什么。他希望他能有机会访问他国家的人民[5]，但是，皇帝出去的时候，常常有许多人跟在他的左右前后[6]。如果人们知道他是皇帝，就不会把真正想要说的话告诉他了，古时候，人民是很怕皇帝的。

所以，皇帝就经常自己一个人出去，或者就带一、两个手下的人，他们穿上老百姓的简单衣服，让自己看起来像一般老百姓的样子。他们不告诉家里人他们要到哪里去，也不告诉别人他们是谁，然后，皇帝就去访问[7]北京城里的老百姓。有时，他还在平民[8]的家里吃饭，皇帝也很喜欢自己一个人去茶馆，和北京的老百姓一起谈天。

因为故宫每天晚上都要关门[9]，晚上到了一定的时间大门就关了，没有人可以随便进出[10]，皇帝因为不想让别人们知道他出去的事情，所以时间一到，他就必须马上回去。

皇帝访问老百姓的事情，最后还是让人知道了，人民都很感谢[11]皇帝这样来访问他们，在中国历史上，有不少这样有趣[12]的故事。

古时候，如果有人来访，要想见皇帝，他先要在一个大门外等候，那个大门叫做"午门[13]"。皇帝的士兵这时会跑进去报告[14]，皇帝同意了，来访的客人才可以和皇帝见面。客人要跟着士兵，走过几个门，然后才能最后见到皇帝。大概，每一个国家的皇帝都一样，这些皇帝都怕来的客人会杀掉[15]皇帝自己。

古代的中国，皇帝在国家里是最大的，皇帝要什么就有什么，想做什么事就可以做什么事，皇帝说的话，人民是不可以不听的。所以，在中国历史上，皇帝是一个影响国家和人民生活最重要的人。

中国历史上的第一个皇帝叫"秦始皇[16]"，那时候，中国不是一个国家，而是七个国家，这七个小国之中，其中有一个叫秦国[17]，秦国的国王很有能力，他的国家虽然小，却统一[18]了当时的整个[19]中国，这在中国历史上是一件很大的事情。

秦国的国王统一了中国后，就不再叫自己是国王了，他叫自己是皇帝，意思就是国王的国王。因为中国古代的皇帝是从他开始的，所以历史上我们又叫他"秦始皇"，他当了皇帝以后，做了很多历史的大事，还建了非常有名的长城。据说[20]，他的皇宫在当时也很大，比现在的故宫还要大很多，可是，秦始皇也做了很多坏事[21]。比如：他不想让人民知道历史，他就烧[22]了全国[23]所有的书，还杀了成千上万[24]的读书人，所以，人民非常恨[25]这个皇帝。秦始皇死了以后，人们还是很恨他，就把他的皇宫烧了，据说这场[26]大火烧了好几天[27]呢！

古时候在中国，每一个皇帝都是从年轻做到年老，死了以后，又让自己的儿子做皇帝，儿子死了以后，儿子的儿子又继续做皇帝。历史上有很多皇帝对人民非常坏，他们不给国家平安，也不给人民幸福，这时，就有人起来把皇帝杀了。杀皇帝的人后来就自己做了皇帝，中国的历史已经有几千年了，其中换[28]了许许多多的皇帝，每一个皇帝都有自己的皇宫，中国的最后一个皇帝也有自己的皇宫，这个皇宫就是现在的故宫。

一九一一年以后，中国就不再有皇帝了。从那以后，故宫就变成了一个博物院[29]，让人们来参观中国古时候的历史、文化、和建筑风格。因为历史上许多皇帝都把北京作为首都，所以在故宫里面就有很多很贵重[30]和稀有[31]的文物，这些文物代表保留着古代的中国文化。现在，每天都有从世界各地来的人们游览参观故宫，故宫成了古代中国历史和文化的一个奇观。

## 阅读理解

1. 故宫在什么地方？
2. 故宫里面是什么样子？
3. 为什么古时候的人民怕皇帝？
4. 皇帝为什么要自己一个人出去访问人民？
5. 中国的第一个皇帝是谁？他做了什么事？
6. 古时候谁可以做皇帝？
7. 从什么时候开始，中国就没有皇帝了？为什么？
8. 古代中国换了多少朝代？多少皇帝？
9. 谈谈你对电影"末代皇帝"的感想。
10. 没有皇帝以后，中国文化有哪些变化？

## 生字

| | | | |
|---|---|---|---|
| 1 | 士兵 | shìbīng | guard |
| 2 | 皇后 | huánghòu | empress |
| 3 | 处理 | chǔlǐ | to handle |
| 4 | 舒服 | shūfú | comfortable |
| 5 | 人民 | rénmín | the people |
| 6 | 左右前后 | zuǒyòuqiánhòu | to be surrounded on all sides. |
| 7 | 访问 | fǎngwèn | to interview |
| 8 | 平民 | píngmín | common |
| 9 | 关门 | guānmén | to lock or close the door |

| | | | |
|---|---|---|---|
| 10 | 进出 | jìnchū | to go in and out |
| 11 | 感谢 | gǎnxiè | to be grateful; to thank |
| 12 | 有趣 | yǒuqù | interesting |
| 13 | 午门 | wǔmén | the gate where visitors waited until they were admitted to the emperor |
| 14 | 报告 | bàogào | to report |
| 15 | 杀掉 | shādiào | to murder; to kill |
| 16 | 秦始皇 | qínshǐhuáng | Qin Shi Huang, the first emperor of China |
| 17 | 秦国 | qínguó | the Kingdom of Qin |
| 18 | 统一 | tǒngyī | to unite |
| 19 | 整个 | zhěnggè | whole; entire |
| 20 | 据说 | jùshuō | legend |
| 21 | 坏事 | huàishì | evil deeds |
| 22 | 烧 | shāo | to burn |
| 23 | 全国 | quánguó | the whole country |
| 24 | 成千上万 | chéngqiānshàngwàn | tens of thousands |
| 25 | 恨 | hèn | to hate |
| 26 | 这场 | zhècháng | measure word; this |
| 27 | 好几天 | hǎojǐtiān | many days |
| 28 | 换 | huàn | to change |
| 29 | 博物院 | bówùyuàn | museum (institute) |
| 30 | 贵重 | guìzhòng | precious |
| 31 | 稀有 | xīyǒu | rare |

# Chapter 4   The Forbidden City

The Forbidden City was the place where the emperor used to live in Beijing, it was also known as the Imperial Palace. Because many of the emperors throughout the past several hundred years chose Beijing as the capital, the Imperial Palace was built there and is now called the Forbidden City. By walking through the big Tian An Men city gate, you can enter the Forbidden City. In order to get to the real living quarters of the emperor, you must walk for quite awhile and pass through many other large gates.

The Forbidden City is made up of a large group of buildings. This group of buildings is inside a very big courtyard. The wall of the courtyard is very high. There are 999 rooms in the courtyard. The reason for this may be that many of the Chinese emperors liked the number nine. There are many houses inside the Forbidden City. Some of the houses are where ordinary people lived who worked for the emperor everyday. Some of the houses are where the guards who protected the emperor lived.

The wife of the emperor was called the empress. The empress and the children lived in their own house with their own courtyard. The emperor's courtyard is very big and there are several special large houses in it. It was here where the emperor held meetings, received all sorts of dignitaries, and handled the important affairs of the country on a daily basis.

In spite of the fact that the Forbidden City was huge and that there were many courtyards and buildings, the emperor did not like living there all the time. He wanted to build more buildings and courtyards in other places as well. This way the emperor could live in more than one place. The buildings and courtyards that the emperor built were not inside Beijing's city walls, they were in an area near Beijing where the landscape was truly beautiful, a place with mountains and lakes. When the weather got hot in the summer, the emperor moved to one of these palaces to live, such as the Summer Palace.

Although the emperor's living quarters were extremely comfortable, he wanted to know how the common people lived. What did they eat? What were their homes like? What did they think about? The emperor wanted to find an opportunity to go out and talk to the people in his country. When the emperor went out, however, he was always surrounded by the people who protected him. Because the common people knew who he was, they would not speak honestly to him. In ancient times, everyone was afraid of the emperor.

So the emperor often went out by himself, taking only one or two servants with him. They put on plain, simple clothes so that they would look like ordinary people. They didn't tell their families where they were going and they didn't tell anyone who they were. The emperor sometimes went to visit the commoners in Beijing and would have a meal in their home. He also enjoyed going to teahouses all by himself in order to chat with ordinary folk.

All the gates in the Forbidden City were locked every night. At a specific time, the great gates were locked and no one could go in or out. Because the emperor didn't want anybody to know about his outings, he had to come home quickly before the gates were locked. In the end, the people did find out that the emperor had been out conversing with the commoners and they were very grateful to him. There are many interesting stories such as these in Chinese history.

In the old days, when someone came to see the emperor, he had to wait outside a large gate. The gate was called "Wu Men." The emperor's guards ran in to report on an arrival. If the emperor permitted, then the visitor could come in and see the emperor. The visitor did, however, have to follow the guards through several more gates until he finally arrived. In general, the emperors of all countries acted like this. They were afraid that the visitor had actually come to commit murder.

In ancient China, the emperor was the most powerful man in the country. If the emperor wanted something, he got it; if the emperor wanted to do something, he did it. When the emperor spoke, the people had to listen and obey. Throughout history, the emperor greatly influenced both the country and its people.

The first emperor of China was called Qin Shi Huang. At that time, China was not one country, it was made up of seven countries. Among these seven small countries was one called the Kingdom of Qin. The King of Qin was a very capable man. Even though his country was very small, he managed to unite China into one whole country. This was a very important event in Chinese history.

After the King of Qin united China, he stopped calling himself king. He called himself emperor instead, which meant king of all kings. Because the line of ancient Chinese emperors started with him, he is called Qin Shi (beginning) Huang. He accomplished many things during his reign, and he also had the famous Great Wall built. According to legend, his palace was very big, much bigger than even the Forbidden City. However, Qin Shi Huang also did things that were wrong. For example, he didn't want his subjects to know about history, so he had all the books in the country burned; he also had tens of thousands of intellectuals killed. He was truly despised because of this. Even after his death, the people still hated Qin Shi Huang and they burned down his imperial palace. It is said that the fire burned for many days.

From those ancient times on, each emperor remained on the throne throughout his life from youth until old age. When an emperor died, his son became emperor. After the son died, the son's son became emperor. Throughout Chinese history, there have been many emperors who were cruel to their people. They didn't bring peace and happiness to their country and their subjects were not happy. There were times when one man rose up and killed the emperor, and after that he was the emperor. The history of China is several thousand years old, and during that time there have been many emperors. Each emperor had his own palace. China's last emperor also had his own palace, which is the one we now call the Forbidden City.

After 1911, there were no more emperors in China. Since then, the Forbidden City has been a museum. It allows people to come and see China's ancient history, its culture, and its architectural styles.

Because Beijing was chosen as the capital by many emperors, the Forbidden City contains a vast amount of precious and rare cultural relics. The relics represent what is left of China's ancient culture. Now there are people from every corner of the globe who come to visit the Forbidden City everyday. The Forbidden City has become a marvel of Chinese history and culture.

# 第五章　北京的老字號和小吃

　　字號就是一個商店的名字,有時也是一個工廠或公司的名字。老字號的意思有二個,一個意思是年代¹很久的意思,比如:有些商店已經有幾百年的歷史了,很多的人從小就聽說這些商店的名字,到了一個人老的時候,這些

商店還在做生意。我們就說：這個商店很老了。老字號的第二個意思是很出名、很有名的商店，這些很有名的商店因為生意老是[2]很好，當然就越來越有名了，老字號也就這樣產生了。

北京的老字號商店已經有差不多一百年的歷史了，在北京和北京附近的地方有很多這樣的商店，它們都是很有特色[3]，很有名的老字號。有些商店不但在北京很有名，在全中國也很有名，還有的商店在國際[4]上也是很受歡迎的。這些商店這麼有名，主要是因為每一家商店都有很多的經驗和各自的特色，每一家老字號都有自己的一個很不容易的歷史。

這些老字號的商店裏，有一些是因為賣中藥出名的，也有一些出名是因為賣書和賣畫。有的老字號商店賣毛筆，有的賣墨水，在這些北京的老字號裏，其中賣吃的飯店是最多的。這些飯店有北方的麵食[5]，南方的炒菜[6]，山東的海鮮[7]，和四川的麻辣[8]。北京很多的老字號飯店都是請客吃飯的好地方，因為那裏的飯菜都很好吃。

在老字號的飯店裏，最有名的可能就是北京烤鴨[9]店了。到北京遊覽的人，一定要吃一吃世界出名的北京烤鴨，北京烤鴨有三種吃法[10]，第一種吃法是主要的吃法，就是吃皮[11]，北京烤鴨的皮非常好吃。紅紅的顏色，脆[12]脆的，味道[13]很香,據說,北京烤鴨可以吃一百片皮,一般烤鴨的皮是用餅[14]包[15]著吃的。第二種吃法是吃肉[16],這個時候,烤鴨肉可以跟米飯一起吃。第三種吃法,就是喝鴨子湯,很多人吃了鴨子皮就已經吃飽了,在北京烤鴨店吃飯,人特別多,也要吃很長的時間。

最有名的北京烤鴨店是一八六四年開始生意的,到今天已經有一百三十多年的歷史了,最開始時,它不是一個烤鴨店,而是一個賣活鴨子的店。後來,這個店的主人開始賣烤鴨,那時候店很小,每天只賣三個菜,可是後來生意越來越好,越做越大,二三十年以後店也變得很大,可以坐兩百多客人,現在,這個烤鴨店已經變成了一個七層[17]樓的大飯店了,它的烤鴨不但是北京第一,也是世界出名的菜。

北京另外一個出名的,就是它有很多的小吃。這些小吃不像老字號飯店,它們沒有什麼名,生意也不大,小吃店不能坐很多人。可是,吃小吃是北京人很平常的生活,不管在路邊[18]還是店裏,你不需要花很多錢,也不需要買很多,隨便走到哪裏,你都可以找一個地方坐下來吃。

北京的小吃店有很長的歷史,也有東西南北[19]各方[20]的很多種吃法。這主要是因為北京是首都,住在北京的各個民族[21]都有。時間一長,各個民族吃的文化就介紹[22]到北京來了。這樣,各個民族你學我的吃法,我學你的做法。

慢慢地,小吃店的東西就越來越好吃。人們也越來越喜歡吃了,結果,北京的小吃店越做越好吃,店就越開越多家,現在,吃小吃店已經成了遊覽北京的人必須要做的一件事情。

這些小吃店在北京到處都是,也有一些人沒有店也賣小吃,他們在街道[23]的兩邊找一個地方,一邊燒東西,一邊叫賣[24]吃的東西,許多時候你在馬路上走路,很容易就會遇見賣小吃的人。有的地方賣小吃的人和買小吃的人太多了,就是走路都不容易走過去,到了這樣的地方,沒有人不想坐下來,買一點東西吃吃,因為吃是人生的一大福氣[25]。

北京這麼多種的小吃,主要是從三個方面介紹進來的。第一是皇宮裏的小吃介紹到了民間[26],變成了民間小吃。第二是許多南方的人來到北京工作,他們就把南方吃的習慣帶到了北京。像元宵[27]和粽子[28]。第三是北方的一些少數民族[29]也把他們各自民族吃的東西帶來了北京。

北京小吃的一個很特別的地方是平民化。北京大多數小吃都很簡單,也不貴,大家吃起來很舒服,很高興。北京小吃的另外一個特別的地方是南方小吃北方化,少數民族小吃北京化，這些外來的小吃改成北京人的口味[30]後，北京的老百姓才會歡迎和接受。

## 閱讀理解

一、什麼叫作老字號？
二、爲什麼每一家老字號都有不容易的歷史？
三、你吃過北京烤鴨嗎？談談你的感受。
四、你喜歡吃中國的小吃嗎？你知道的有那些種？
五、北京小吃是怎麼來的？
六、你喜歡吃中國菜嗎？你知道怎麼做的嗎？
七、什麼叫作平民化？
八、中國南方吃的習慣和北方有那些不一樣？

# 生字

| | | | | |
|---|---|---|---|---|
| 1 | 年代 | niándài | ㄋㄧㄢˊ ㄉㄞˋ | time; age |
| 2 | 老是 | lǎoshì | ㄌㄠˇ ㄕˋ | always |
| 3 | 特色 | tèsè | ㄊㄜˋ ㄙㄜˋ | distinguished |
| 4 | 國際 | guójì | ㄍㄨㄛˊ ㄐㄧˋ | international |
| 5 | 麵食 | miànshí | ㄇㄧㄢˋ ㄕˊ | products made from wheat |
| 6 | 炒菜 | chǎocài | ㄔㄠˇ ㄘㄞˋ | fried dishes |
| 7 | 海鮮 | hǎixiān | ㄏㄞˇ ㄒㄧㄢ | seafood |
| 8 | 麻辣 | málà | ㄇㄚˊ ㄌㄚˋ | spices |
| 9 | 烤鴨 | kǎoyā | ㄎㄠˇ ㄧㄚ | roast duck |
| 10 | 吃法 | chīfǎ | ㄔ ㄈㄚˇ | eating methods |
| 11 | 皮 | pí | ㄆㄧˊ | skin |
| 12 | 脆 | cuì | ㄘㄨㄟˋ | crisp |
| 13 | 味道 | wèidào | ㄨㄟˋ ㄉㄠˋ | taste; flavor |
| 14 | 餅 | bǐng | ㄅㄧㄥˇ | pancake |
| 15 | 包 | bāo | ㄅㄠ | to wrap |
| 16 | 肉 | ròu | ㄖㄡˋ | meat |
| 17 | 層 | céng | ㄘㄥˊ | story; lager |
| 18 | 路邊 | lùbiān | ㄌㄨˋ ㄅㄧㄢ | along the street |
| 19 | 東西南北 | dōngxīnánběi | ㄉㄨㄥ ㄒㄧ ㄋㄢˊ ㄅㄟˇ | all directions; everywhere |
| 20 | 各方 | gèfāng | ㄍㄜˋ ㄈㄤ | various places |
| 21 | 民族 | mínzú | ㄇㄧㄣˊ ㄗㄨˊ | nationalities |

| | | | | |
|---|---|---|---|---|
| 22 | 介紹 | jièshào | ㄐㄧㄝˋ ㄕㄠˋ | to introduce |
| 23 | 街道 | jiēdào | ㄐㄧㄝ ㄉㄠˋ | street |
| 24 | 叫賣 | jiàomài | ㄐㄧㄠˋ ㄇㄞˋ | to hawk; to sell |
| 25 | 福氣 | fúqì | ㄈㄨˊ ㄑㄧˋ | a blessing |
| 26 | 民間 | mínjiān | ㄇㄧㄣˊ ㄐㄧㄢ | popular |
| 27 | 元宵 | yuánxiāo | ㄩㄢˊ ㄒㄧㄠ | sweet dumplings (for the Lantern Festival) |
| 28 | 粽子 | zòngzi | ㄗㄨㄥˋ ㄗ˙ | pyramid-shaped dumplings (for the Dragon Boat Festival) |
| 29 | 少數民族 | shǎoshùmínzú | ㄕㄠˇ ㄕㄨˋ ㄇㄧㄣˊ ㄗㄨˊ | national minorities |
| 30 | 口味 | kǒuwèi | ㄎㄡˇ ㄨㄟˋ | taste |

# 第五章　北京的老字号和小吃

字号就是一个商店的名字，有时也是一个工厂或公司的名字。老字号的意思有二个，一个意思是年代[1]很久的意思，比如：有些商店已经有几百年的历史了，很多的人从小就听说这些商店的名字，到了一个人老的时候，这些商店还在做生意。我们就说：这个商店很老了。老字号的第二个意思是很出名、很有名的商店，这些很有名的商店因为生意老是[2]很好，当然就越来越有名了，老字号也就这样产生了。

北京的老字号商店已经有差不多一百年的历史了，在北京和北京附近的地方有很多这样的商店，它们都是很有特色[3]，很有名的老字号。有些商店不但在北京很有名，在全中国也很有名，还有的商店在国际[4]上也是很受欢迎的。这些商店这么有名，主要是因为每一家商店都有很多的经验和各自的特色，每一家老字号都有自己的一个很不容易的历史。

这些老字号的商店里，有一些是因为卖中药出名的，也有一些出名是因为卖书和卖画。有的老字号商店卖毛笔，有的卖墨水，在这些北京的老字号里，其中卖吃的饭店是最多的。这些饭店有北方的面食[5]，南方的炒菜[6]，山东的海鲜[7]，和四川的麻辣[8]。北京很多的老字号饭店都是请客吃饭的好地方，因为那里的饭菜都很好吃。

在老字号的饭店里，最有名的可能就是北京烤鸭[9]店了。到北京游览的人，一定要吃一吃世界出名的北京烤鸭，北京烤鸭有三种吃法[10]，第一种吃法是主要的吃法，就是吃皮[11]，北京烤鸭的皮非常好吃。红红的颜色，脆[12]脆的，味道[13]很香，据说，北京烤鸭可以吃一百片皮，一般烤鸭的皮是用饼[14]包[15]着吃的。第二种吃法是吃肉[16]，这个时候，烤鸭肉可以跟米饭一起吃。第三种吃法，就是喝鸭子汤，很多人吃了鸭子皮就已经吃饱了，在北京烤鸭店吃饭，人特别多，也要吃很长的时间。

最有名的北京烤鸭店是一八六四年开始生意的，到今天已经有一百三十多年的历史了，最开始时，它不是一个烤鸭店，而是一个卖活鸭子的店。后来，这个店的主人开始卖烤鸭，那时候店很小，每天只卖三个菜，可是后来生意越来越好，越做越大，二三十年以后店也变得很大，可以坐两百多客人，现在，这个烤鸭店已经变成了一个七层

[17]楼的大饭店了,它的烤鸭不但是北京第一,也是世界出名的菜。

北京另外一个出名的,就是它有很多的小吃。这些小吃不像老字号饭店,它们没有什么名,生意也不大,小吃店不能坐很多人。可是,吃小吃是北京人很平常的生活,不管在路边[18]还是店里,你不需要花很多钱,也不需要买很多,随便走到哪里,你都可以找一个地方坐下来吃。

北京的小吃店有很长的历史,也有东西南北[19]各方[20]的很多种吃法。这主要是因为北京是首都,住在北京的各个民族[21]都有。时间一长,各个民族吃的文化就介绍[22]到北京来了。这样,各个民族你学我的吃法,我学你的做法。

慢慢地,小吃店的东西就越来越好吃。人们也越来越喜欢吃了,结果,北京的小吃店越做越好吃,店就越开越多家,现在,吃小吃店已经成了游览北京的人必须要做的一件事情。

这些小吃店在北京到处都是,也有一些人没有店也卖小吃,他们在街道[23]的两边找一个地方,一边烧东西,一边叫卖[24]吃的东西,许多时候你在马路上走路,很容易就会遇见卖小吃的人。有的地方卖小吃的人和买小吃的人太多了,就是走路都不容易走过去,到了这样的地方,没有人不想坐下来，买一点东西吃吃，因为吃是人生的一大福气[25]。

北京这么多种的小吃，主要是从三个方面介绍进来的。第一是皇宫里的小吃介绍到了民间[26]，变成了民间小吃。第二是许多南方的人来到北京工作，他们就把南方吃的习惯带到了北京。像元宵[27]和粽子[28]。第三是北方的一些少数民族[29]也把他们各自民族吃的东西带来了北京。

北京小吃的一个很特别的地方是平民化。北京大多数小吃都很简单，也不贵，大家吃起来很舒服，很高兴。北京小吃的另外一个特别的地方是南方小吃北方化，少数民族小吃北京化，这些外来的小吃改成北京人的口味[30]后，北京的老百姓才会欢迎和接受。

## 阅读理解

1. 什么叫作老字号？
2. 为什么每一家老字号都有不容易的历史？
3. 你吃过北京烤鸭吗？谈谈你的感受。
4. 你喜欢吃中国的小吃吗？你知道的有那些种？
5. 北京小吃是怎么来的？
6. 你喜欢吃中国菜吗？你知道怎么做的吗？
7. 什么叫作平民化？
8. 中国南方吃的习惯和北方有那些不一样？

# 生字

1. 年代　niándài　time; age
2. 老是　lǎoshì　always
3. 特色　tèsè　distinguished
4. 国际　guójì　international
5. 面食　miànshí　products made from wheat
6. 炒菜　chǎocài　fried dishes
7. 海鲜　hǎixiān　seafood
8. 麻辣　málà　spices
9. 烤鸭　kǎoyā　roast duck
10. 吃法　chīfǎ　eating methods
11. 皮　pí　skin
12. 脆　cuì　crisp
13. 味道　wèidào　taste; flavor
14. 饼　bǐng　pancake
15. 包　bāo　to wrap
16. 肉　ròu　meat
17. 层　céng　story; lager
18. 路边　lùbiān　along the street
19. 东西南北　dōngxīnánběi　all directions; everywhere
20. 各方　gèfāng　various places
21. 民族　mínzú　nationalities
22. 介绍　jièshào　to introduce
23. 街道　jiēdào　street
24. 叫卖　jiàomài　to hawk; to sell
25. 福气　fúqì　a blessing
26. 民间　mínjiān　popular
27. 元宵　yuánxiāo　sweet dumplings (for the Lantern Festival)
28. 粽子　zòngzi　pyramid-shaped dumplings (for the Dragon Boat Festival)
29. 少数民族　shǎoshùmínzú　national minorities
30. 口味　kǒuwèi　taste

# Chapter 5  Famous Old Stores and Snack Bars

"Zi Hao" means "store," sometimes it is also the name of a factory or a company. There are two meanings to the word "Lao Zi Hao." One definition is "very old." For example, if a store has a history of several hundred years, or if many people have heard the name of a business all their life and the store is still in business when they are old, we call that kind of store "old." The second meaning of "Lao Zi Hao" is "well-known" or "famous." Because business was always good in these stores, they obviously became more and more famous and that is how the Old Famous Stores emerged.

Beijing's Old famous Stores have a history of about 100 years. There are many such stores in and around Beijing. The Old Famous Stores are very distinguished and very famous. Some of the stores are not only known in Beijing, but all across the country. Some of them are also well-known abroad. The main reason for the stores' fame is their experience and individual character. Each store also has a history full of hardships.

Among these famous stores are some that became famous for selling Chinese medicine. Others became famous for their books and paintings. Still other Old Famous Stores sell paint brushes, some sell ink. The greatest number of Old Famous Stores are restaurants which sell food. The restaurants sell northern products made from wheat, southern fried dishes, seafood from Shandong, and spicy dishes from

Si Chuan. The Old Famous Restaurants are good places to invite friends because of their delicious food.

Among the Old Famous Restaurants, the most well-known is probably the Beijing Duck Restaurant. Tourists visiting Beijing ought to try the world renowned Beijing Duck.

There are three methods of eating Beijing Duck. The first and most popular consists of eating the skin. The roasted duck's skin is extremely delicious. It is red and crisp and very fragrant. Some say that each duck can yield 100 pieces of skin. Generally, the skin is wrapped into a kind of pancake. The second method is eating the meat of the duck, which can be eaten with rice. The third is duck soup. Duck skin fills many people, however, and they never get to the second or third ways of eating duck. The Beijing Duck Restaurant is always very crowded and it takes a long time to eat a meal there.

The most famous Beijing Duck Restaurant was established in 1864. It has been in business for over 130 years. In the beginning, it wasn't a Beijing Duck restaurant, instead it sold live ducks. Later on, the owner of the store started selling roast ducks. The store was very small at the time and the owner sold only three dishes per day. Business got better and better the more they worked, and the bigger the store got. Within ten to twenty years, the store had changed a lot and could seat more than 200 people. The roast duck restaurant has now evolved into a seven-story restaurant. Not only does it serve the best roast duck in Beijing, but it has also become known throughout the world.

Another famous aspect of Beijing is its many street-side snack bars. The snack bars are not like the Old Famous Stores. They are not famous at all and business is minimal. They only seat a few customers. But eating in these snack bars is part of ordinary life in Beijing. Whether they are along the street or inside a building, the snack bars are cheap and one needn't buy large amounts. One can stroll around and look for a table to sit at and eat.

The Beijing snack bars have been around for a long time and they sell a variety of food from all corners of the country. The main reason for this is that Beijing is the capital and people from all different nationalities live there. Over time, the eating customs of the different nationalities were adopted in Beijing as people learned about one another's customs.

Slowly but surely the food served in the snack bars improved. People also enjoyed eating there more and more. As a result, the food in Beijing's snack bars got better and better and more of them opened up. Snack bars have become a "must do" for tourists visiting Beijing.

Snack bars are everywhere in Beijing. Some vendors don't even have a shop, but they still sell snacks. They find a place on either side of the street where they cook and sell their food. While walking along the streets you can see people selling food everywhere. In some areas, there are so many people selling and buying snacks that it is difficult to pass. People walking through those areas can't resist sitting down, buying a few things and eating them. Eating is one of life's great blessings.

Beijing's many different snacks have three main origins. The first is the food that originated in the Imperial Palace and was introduced to the people and turned into popular snacks. The second influence is from the many southerners who came to work in Beijing. They brought southern eating customs with them. Southerners introduced the sweet dumplings eaten during the Lantern Festival and the pyramid-shaped dumplings eaten during the Dragon Boat Festival. The third influence came from all the minorities who each brought their specialties with them to Beijing.

The popularity of Beijing's street-side snack bars is quite extraordinary. Most of the snack bars serve simple, inexpensive food and the customers feel good and happy. Another aspect that makes the Beijing snack bars so special is that southern cooking was adjusted to suit the northern palate, and snacks served by minorities were adjusted to suit the taste of the Beijing citizens. When the dishes introduced from afar had been adjusted to suit the Beijing palate, the people of Beijing accepted and welcomed them.

# 第六章　頤和園和長城

　　頤和園其實就是一個花園，是皇帝最大的一個花園。這個花園很大，即使你用一天的時間也是不可能看完裏面

的風景，頤和園十分美麗，人到了頤和園就像走進了一幅畫裏一樣[1]，久久不願意[2]離開。

　　古時候，皇帝經常在夏天來到這裏辦事[3]和休息，所以頤和園也叫夏宮[4]。一到夏天，皇帝一定要到頤和園來住一些時候，為了讓頤和園這個地方在夏天更涼快，皇帝特別在頤和園裏建了一座人工湖，叫作"昆明湖[5]"。意思是，一年四季都像春天一樣舒服，昆明湖很大，頤和園四分之三[6]的地方都是昆明湖的湖水，在昆明湖的中間，有一座山，山上有休息的地方，從這座山到湖邊，有一座橋可以走過去。

　　頤和園裏很有名的一個風景是石船[7]，這個石船是用大理石[8]做的，有三十六米[9]長，分[10]上、下兩層，從船上看去，可以看到湖面很遠，頤和園的另一個有名的風景是長廊[11]，這個長廊有七百多米長，是中國最長的長廊，長廊分成一間[12]一間的，一共有二百七十三間，位於[13]昆明湖的北邊，從長廊去看昆明湖，十分的美麗，如果從湖裏的小船上來看長廊，也是非常好看的。

　　每年夏天，皇帝來頤和園休息的時候，都要在這裏看京劇，有的時候，要看幾天，演京劇的地方很大，皇帝很喜歡看京劇，常常在北京的三個地方看，其中一個是故宮，而頤和園算是這三個看京劇的地方裏最大的。

從北京往北走，就是中國最有名的長城，長城是一座很長很長的牆，這是秦始皇為了保護自己的國家，就在當時中國最北邊的地方建的這座牆，這座牆後來的人叫它"長城"。長城有幾十米高，比古代一般的城牆還要高很多，長城的上面可以走路，上面和現代城市[14]裏的馬路一樣寬[15]，在長城上面走，每走一段[16]路就有一座門樓[17]。

古時候，皇帝每年都要派很多的士兵到長城，皇帝派來的士兵就住在這裏保護中國，每一次如果發現有什麼問題，或者是要打仗了，人們就在長城上燒一種東西，這種東西叫"狼煙[18]"，在燒狼煙時，狼煙會放出很多的煙[19]來，這種煙會一直飄[20]到天空都不會散掉，遠處[21]的人就可以根據煙的大小判斷敵人來了多少，這樣遠近的人們都可以知道這個消息。

長城有幾千公里[22]長，用了許多人工，花費[23]了許多的錢和很多年的時間才完成，長城大部分是建在山上的高處[24]，到了長城，你一定會奇怪地問，幾千年前，中國人怎麼會這麼聰明，建造[25]這麼大的歷史建築，真是一個奇觀。

長城已經有幾千年的的歷史了，因為自然的變化，現在，古長城的許多地方已經壞了。在北京附近的這一段長城，是現在保護得最好也是最美麗的一段長城。在這一段長城上，有八個門樓，而且一個門樓比一個門樓高，雖然人們在長城上可以走路，可是因為長城是建在山上，走路非常不容易。常常需要在每一門樓的地方休息一下，然後再繼續走，不過，當你走上長城最高的地方的時候，你可以看到長城最美麗的風景。這時，你會發現，長城真是很長，從你的前面一直到很遠很遠，好像看不到長城是從哪裏出來，一直要到哪裏去。

長城很有名，是中國古代歷史和文化的一個象徵。所以，許多來中國訪問的外國元首，如：美國前總統[26]尼克松[27](Richard M. Nixon)和布什[28](George Bush)都上過長城，來北京遊覽的人，一定要去長城，要不然他們會覺得好像沒有到過北京，中國有一句古話，叫作"不到長城非好漢"，意思是，如果你還沒有去過長城，應該在自己人生在世[29]的日子裏，去一次長城。這樣，你才是完成了人生的一件大事。

也許是因為古時候的這一句話，現在來長城的人越來越多，有的時候，你會覺得在長城上的人太多了，好像長城不再是石頭[30]建的城牆，而是很大的一座人牆[31]。在長城上的人不一定都是已經完成了人生大事的人，但是，人人看起來都像是要做大事的人。在長城上，你可以看到中國的過去，同時，你好像也看到了中國的將來。

# 閱讀理解

一、你去過長城和頤和園嗎？說說你的感受。
二、頤和園以前是作什麼用的？現在是作什麼用的？
三、頤和園的風景有哪些？
四、以前皇帝在什麼地方看京劇？
五、長城有多長？有多大？
六、長城以前是作什麼用的？現在是作什麼用的？

# 生字

| | | | | |
|---|---|---|---|---|
| 1 | 幅 | fú | ㄈㄨˊ | measure word for picture |
| 2 | 願意 | yuànyì | ㄩㄢˋㄧˋ | to want to; to be willing to |
| 3 | 辦事 | bànshì | ㄅㄢˋㄕˋ | to take care of business; to handle; to manage |
| 4 | 夏宮 | xiàgōng | ㄒㄧㄚˋㄍㄨㄥ | Summer Palace |
| 5 | 昆明湖 | kūnmínghú | ㄎㄨㄣㄇㄧㄥˊㄏㄨˊ | Kunming Lake (at the Summer Palace) |
| 6 | 四分之三 | sìfēnzhīsān | ㄙˋㄈㄣㄓㄙㄢ | three quarters |
| 7 | 石船 | shíchuán | ㄕˊㄔㄨㄢˊ | Stone Boat |
| 8 | 大理石 | dàlǐshí | ㄉㄚˋㄌㄧˇㄕˊ | marble |
| 9 | 米 | mǐ | ㄇㄧˇ | meter |
| 10 | 分 | fēn | ㄈㄣ | divided |

| | | | | |
|---|---|---|---|---|
| 11 | 長廊 | chángláng | ㄔㄤˊ ㄌㄤˊ | Long Corridor |
| 12 | 間 | jiān | ㄐㄧㄢ | section |
| 13 | 位於 | wèiyú | ㄨㄟˋ ㄩˊ | located at |
| 14 | 城市 | chéngshì | ㄔㄥˊ ㄕˋ | city |
| 15 | 寬 | kuān | ㄎㄨㄢ | wide |
| 16 | 段 | duàn | ㄉㄨㄢˋ | a section |
| 17 | 門樓 | ménlóu | ㄇㄣˊ ㄌㄡˊ | guard house |
| 18 | 狼煙 | lángyān | ㄌㄤˊ ㄧㄢ | wolves dung burnt at border posts to signal alarm |
| 19 | 煙 | yān | ㄧㄢ | smoke |
| 20 | 飄 | piāo | ㄆㄧㄠ | to scatter; to drift |
| 21 | 遠處 | yuǎnchù | ㄩㄢˇ ㄔㄨˋ | distant places |
| 22 | 公里 | gōnglǐ | ㄍㄨㄥ ㄌㄧˇ | kilometers |
| 23 | 花費 | huāfèi | ㄏㄨㄚ ㄈㄟˋ | expenses |
| 24 | 高處 | gāochù | ㄍㄠ ㄔㄨˋ | elevated areas |
| 25 | 建造 | jiànzào | ㄐㄧㄢˋ ㄗㄠˋ | to build |
| 26 | 前總統 | qiánzǒngtǒng | ㄑㄧㄢˊ ㄗㄨㄥˇ ㄊㄨㄥˇ | former president |
| 27 | 尼克松 | níkèsōng | ㄋㄧˊ ㄎㄜˋ ㄙㄨㄥ | Nixon |
| 28 | 布什 | bùshí | ㄅㄨˋ ㄕˊ | Bush |
| 29 | 人生在世 | rénshēngzàishì | ㄖㄣˊ ㄕㄥ ㄗㄞˋ ㄕˋ | life in this world |
| 30 | 石頭 | shítóu | ㄕˊ ㄊㄡˊ | stone |
| 31 | 人牆 | rénqiáng | ㄖㄣˊ ㄑㄧㄤˊ | wall of people |

# 第六章　颐和园和长城

颐和园其实就是一个花园,是皇帝最大的一个花园。这个花园很大,即使你用一天的时间也是不可能看完里面的风景,颐和园十分美丽,人到了颐和园就像走进了一幅画里一样[1],久久不愿意[2]离开。

古时候,皇帝经常在夏天来到这里办事[3]和休息,所以颐和园也叫夏宫[4]。一到夏天,皇帝一定要到颐和园来住一些时候,为了让颐和园这个地方在夏天更凉快,皇帝特别在颐和园里建了一座人工湖,叫作"昆明湖[5]"。意思是,一年四季都像春天一样舒服,昆明湖很大,颐和园四分之三[6]的地方都是昆明湖的湖水,在昆明湖的中间,有一座山,山上有休息的地方,从这座山到湖边,有一座桥可以走过去。

颐和园里很有名的一个风景是石船[7],这个石船是用大理石[8]做的,有三十六米[9]长,分[10]上、下两层,从船上看去，可以看到湖面很远，颐和园的另一个有名的风景是长廊[11]，这个长廊有七百多米长，是中国最长的长廊，长廊分成一间[12]一间的，一共有二百七十三间，位于[13]昆明湖的北边，从长廊去看昆明湖，十分的美丽，如果从湖里的小船上来看长廊，也是非常好看的。

每年夏天，皇帝来颐和园休息的时候，都要在这里看京剧，有的时候，要看几天，演京剧的地方很大，皇帝很喜欢看京剧，常常在北京的三个地方看，其中一个是故宫，而颐和园算是这三个看京剧的地方里最大的。

从北京往北走，就是中国最有名的长城，长城是一座很长很长的墙，这是秦始皇为了保护自己的国家，就在当时中国最北边的地方建的这座墙，这座墙后来的人叫它"长城"。长城有几十米高，比古代一般的城墙还要高很多，长城的上面可以走路，上面和现代城市[14]里的马路一样宽[15]，在长城上面走，每走一段[16]路就有一座门楼[17]。

古时候，皇帝每年都要派很多的士兵到长城，皇帝派来的士兵就住在这里保护中国，每一次如果发现有什么问题，或者是要打仗了，人们就在长城上烧一种东西，这种东西叫"狼烟[18]"，在烧狼烟时，狼烟会放出很多的烟[19]来，这种烟会一直飘[20]到天空都不会散掉，远处[21]的人就可以根据烟的大小判断敌人来了多少，这样远近的人们都可以知道这个消息。

长城有几千公里[22]长，用了许多人工，花费[23]了许多的钱和很多年的时间才完成，长城大部分是建在山上的高处[24]，到了长城，你一定会奇怪地问，几千年前，中国人怎么会这么聪明，建造[25]这么大的历史建筑，真是一个奇观。

长城已经有几千年的的历史了，因为自然的变化，现在，古长城的许多地方已经坏了。在北京附近的这一段长城，是现在保护得最好也是最美丽的一段长城。在这一段长城上，有八个门楼，而且一个门楼比一个门楼高，虽然人们在长城上可以走路，可是因为长城是建在山上，走路非常不容易。常常需要在每一门楼的地方休息一下，然后再继续走，不过，当你走上长城最高的地方的时候，你可以看到长城最美丽的风景。这时，你会发现，长城真是很长，从你的前面一直到很远很远，好像看不到长城是从哪里出来，一直要到哪里去。

长城很有名，是中国古代历史和文化的一个象征。所以，许多来中国访问的外国元首，如：美国前总统[26]尼克松[27](Richard M. Nixon)和布什[28](George Bush)都上过长城，来北京游览的人，一定要去长城，要不然他们会觉得好像没有到过北京，中国有一句古话，叫作"不到长城非好汉"，意思是，如果你还没有去过长城，应该在自己人生在世[29]的日子里，去一次长城。这样，你才是完成了人生的一件大事。

也许是因为古时候的这一句话，现在来长城的人越来越多，有的时候，你会觉得在长城上的人太多了，好像长城不再是石头[30]建的城墙，而是很大的一座人墙[31]。在长城上的人不一定都是已经完成了人生大事的人，但是，人人看起来都像是要做大事的人。在长城上，你可以看到中国的过去，同时，你好像也看到了中国的将来。

## 阅读理解

1. 你去过长城和颐和园吗？说说你的感受。
2. 颐和园以前是作什么用的？现在是作什么用的？
3. 颐和园的风景有哪些？
4. 以前皇帝在什么地方看京剧？
5. 长城有多长？有多大？
6. 长城以前是作什么用的？现在是作什么用的？

## 生字

| | | | |
|---|---|---|---|
| 1 | 幅 | fú | *measure word for picture* |
| 2 | 愿意 | yuànyì | *to want to; to be willing to* |
| 3 | 办事 | bànshì | *to take care of business* |

| | | | |
|---|---|---|---|
| 4 | 夏官 | xiàgōng | Summer Palace |
| 5 | 昆明湖 | kūnmínghú | Kunming Lake (at the Summer Palace) |
| 6 | 四分之三 | sìfēnzhīsān | three quarters |
| 7 | 石船 | shíchuán | Stone Boat |
| 8 | 大理石 | dàlǐshí | marble |
| 9 | 米 | mǐ | meter |
| 10 | 分 | fēn | divided |
| 11 | 长廊 | chángláng | Long Corridor |
| 12 | 间 | jiān | section |
| 13 | 位于 | wèiyú | located |
| 14 | 城市 | chéngshì | city |
| 15 | 宽 | kuān | wide |
| 16 | 段 | duàn | a section |
| 17 | 门楼 | ménlóu | guard house |
| 18 | 狼烟 | lángyān | wolves dung burnt at border posts to signal alarm |
| 19 | 烟 | yān | smoke |
| 20 | 飘 | piāo | to scatter; to drift |
| 21 | 远处 | yuǎnchù | distant places |
| 22 | 公里 | gōnglǐ | kilometers |
| 23 | 花费 | huāfèi | expenses |
| 24 | 高处 | gāochù | elevated areas |
| 25 | 建造 | jiànzào | to build |
| 26 | 前总统 | qiánzǒngtǒng | former president |
| 27 | 尼克松 | níkèsōng | Nixon |
| 28 | 布什 | bùshí | Bush |
| 29 | 人生在世 | rénshēngzàishì | life in this world |
| 30 | 石头 | shítóu | stone |
| 31 | 人墙 | rénqiáng | wall of people |

# Chapter 6   The Summer Palace and the Great Wall

The Summer Palace is actually a garden, it was once the emperor's biggest garden. The garden is so big that even in one whole day it is not possible to see all the sights. The Summer Palace is really very pretty. When visitors arrive, they feel as if they have stepped into a painting and they never want to leave again.

In ancient times, the emperor often spent his summers there to take care of his affairs and relax. That is how this palace got its name. In the summer, the emperor always spent some time in the Summer Palace. In order to make the Summer Palace even more refreshing, the emperor had an artificial lake built there.  It is called Kunming Lake, which means that all year round the weather is as comfortable as in springtime. Kunming Lake is very big, three quarters of the palace grounds are covered by it. In the middle of Kunming Lake is a mountain and on that mountain is a place for resting. There is a bridge between the mountain and the shore for crossing.

One of the best-known sights in the Summer Palace is the Stone Boat. The boat is thirty-six meters long, divided into an upper and lower level, and made of marble. Standing on the boat one can see very far. Another very famous sight at the Summer Palace is the Long Corridor. The corridor is more than 700 meters long, the longest corridor in China. The Long Corridor is separated into sections, all together there are 273 sections. The corridor is located along the northern shore of Kunming Lake. Looking at Kunming Lake from the Long Corridor is a lovely sight. Looking at the Long Corridor from a small boat on the lake is also very pretty.

Every summer when the emperor was at the Summer Palace, he watched Beijing Opera. Sometimes he watched for several days. The Beijing Opera stage was very big. The emperor liked watching Beijing Opera very much and he spent a lot of time at the three theaters in Beijing. One of the three was inside the Forbidden City. However, the stage at the Summer Palace was the biggest of all.

Toward the north of Beijing lies the famous Great Wall of China. The Great Wall is a very, very long wall. Qin Shi Huang built the wall to protect what was then China's northern border region. Later, people called the wall the Great Wall. The Great Wall is several dozen meters high, much higher, in those days, than an ordinary wall. One can walk along the top of the Great Wall, it is as wide as a modern city street. Every so often, along the top of the wall, there is a guard house.

In olden days, the emperor sent many soldiers to the Great Wall. They were sent there by the emperor to protect China. Whenever an incident occurred or fighting broke out, the soldiers set fire to dried dung on top of the wall. The burning dung made a big cloud of smoke which rose to the sky without drifting away. People far away could assess the number of enemies by the size of the smoke signal. It was a way for people far and near to be informed of the news.

The Great Wall is several thousand kilometers long. It took a lot of manpower, enormous expenses, and many years to finish. For the most part, the Great Wall was built high in the mountains. When you arrive at the Great Wall, you will surely wonder how, several thousand years ago, the Chinese had the ability to build such a wall. This ancient structure is truly a wonder.

The Great Wall is already several thousand years old. Because of natural erosion, many parts of the ancient wall are already broken. The section of the wall nearest to Beijing is the best preserved section. It is also the most beautiful part of the Great Wall. Along this short section there are eight guard houses, each one higher than the last. Although it is possible to walk along the top of the Great Wall, it is not at all easy because the wall was built in the mountains. It is often necessary to rest at a guard house before continuing the ascent. However, when you do reach the highest point, you will be able to see the most beautiful landscape surrounding the Great Wall and you will realize that the Great Wall is really very long. Looking in front of you into the far distance, you won't be able to see where the wall came from and how far it goes.

The Great Wall of China is very famous, it is the historical and cultural symbol of China. Many visiting foreign heads of state, including former U.S. Presidents Nixon and Bush, have climbed the Great Wall. Tourists visiting Beijing must all go to the Great Wall or it may seem as if they never arrived in Beijing. There is a Chinese proverb: "If you have not visited the Great Wall, you are not a hero." The meaning of this proverb is that if you haven't been to the Great Wall, you ought to go there while you are still living in this world. Only then will you accomplish something significant in your life.

It is probably due to this ancient proverb that more and more people visit the Great Wall. At times you may feel that the Great Wall is too crowded. It may feel as if the Great Wall is not a wall constructed of stone, but rather a wall made of humans. The people on the Great Wall are not necessarily people who have accomplished something significant in their lives, but they all look as if they wanted to accomplish something. At the Great Wall one can see China's past and, simultaneously, maybe even its future.

# 第七章　王府井大街和變化中的
消費生活

王府井[1]大街是北京最有名的商業區，它從南面的長安街開始，到北面的中國美術館[2]，一共大約有三華里[3]路那麼長。大概在一千年前，這裏不過是一個名不見經傳[4]的小地方，後來，這裏的人越來越多，據說，是因為曾經[5]有十個地方的王就住在這裏，他們建了十座很漂亮的王宮，王宮也叫做王府。所以，後來人們就把這裏叫做王府井。

　　從那以後，王府井就有人在做生意了，開始的時候多半是賣帽子[6]的生意。後來有人開起了簡單的小店。日子久了，各種小店越來越多，最後變成了一個很大的市場[7]。慢慢地，全國各地的東西都運[8]到這裏來賣。

　　到了一九〇〇年，王府井已經是北京一個很熱鬧的地方了。當時，王府井附近常常有燈市[9]。因為燈市很出名，所以遊覽的人特別多。這樣，來王府井的人也就多了。人們看完燈市就到王府井來買東西。慢慢地，這裏成了一個很大的商業區。二十年代的時候，許多的外國商人也在這裏開始各種的業務[10]。所以，王府井許多的商店都很老了，有的是幾十年，還有的是一百多年的歷史了。

　　從五十年代開始，王府井大街有了很大的發展和變化。許多新的商業中心[11]建起來了，商店和廣告到處都是。

每天來到這裏的人群像流水[12]一樣，最多的時候差不多有一百萬[13]人。

王府井的許多商店差不多都是最有名的。這裏有北京烤鴨店，中國第一有名的中藥房、和許許多多的老字號。現在，王府井大街是北京最古老、最有名、也是最熱鬧的三大商業中心之一。

但是，中國的商業發展為什麼這麼慢呢？中國文化有幾千年的歷史，而商業的發展卻是在近代[14]的事。這是因為，在古時候中國文化對商業是很不重視的。不但不重視，反而認為商業對社會和人民的思想不一定有好處[15]。古時候的中國人認為，商業會使人變得自私，而太多的自私常常會使人和人之間變得非常緊張。這樣，國家和社會就容易發生很多的問題。

因為這個原因，中國人幾千年來的生活一直非常簡單，也沒有很多的變化。傳統的觀念告訴人們，只要有飯吃，有衣服穿和有書讀，一個人的生活就是很幸福了。結果，中國社會一直發展很慢。中國人的生活一直也是很低[16]的。

只是到了最近的二十年，中國人的思想才有了很大的變化。特別是因為看到了西方社會的發展，中國人才感到商業對現代的中國社會是非常重要的。因為這個原因，政府開始接受西方國家的一些觀念，重視商業在中國的發展。

近幾年來，中國發生了很大的變化。人民的生活越來越好。電視[17]已經成了每個家庭生活的重要一部分。越來越多的中國家庭已經有了電話。同時，中國人對錢的觀念開始有了很大的變化。以前，中國人的觀念是有錢不花錢。雖然有錢，可是不把錢拿出來用。結果，生活得很辛苦，很累。現在，很多人的看法變了。人們覺得，錢是給人用的，而不是人給錢用的。應該花的錢是不能不花的。

另外，中國人花錢的方式[18]也有了變化。以前人們的錢主要是花在吃飯和穿衣服這兩件事情上，很少花在其他的方面。現在，許多人開始注意花錢在教育和旅遊[19]這一些方面。以前，中國人對吃飯是不隨便的。吃飯一定要吃熱的，要有幾個菜，一個湯。現在，很多人已經接受了快餐的概念。快餐非常簡單，也很便宜[20]。世界上最大的"麥當勞[21]快餐廳"就在王府井大街。

王府井大街的發展，是北京人生活變化的象徵。現代商業文化已經成了北京人文化生活的一個重要部分。在王府井大街上，你也許可以看見北京人現代生活的明天。

## 閱讀理解

一、王府井大街是怎麼來的？
二、為什麼王府井大街會成為一個商業中心？
三、最開始王府井的名字是什麼意思？
四、王府井有多少年的歷史？
五、中國歷史上的商業為什發展很慢？
六、最近二十年來，中國的商業有什麼發展和變化？
七、中國人的消費生活有那些變化？
八、為什麼中國人現在喜歡西方的消費方式？

## 生字

| | | | | |
|---|---|---|---|---|
| 1 | 王府井 | wángfǔjǐng | ㄨㄤˊ ㄈㄨˇ ㄐㄧㄥˇ | Wang Fu Jin, a shopping street in Beijing |
| 2 | 中國美術館 | zhōngguó měishùguǎn | ㄓㄨㄥ ㄍㄨㄛˊ ㄇㄟˇ ㄕㄨˋ ㄍㄨㄢˇ | Chinese Gallery of Fine Arts |
| 3 | 華里 | huálǐ | ㄏㄨㄚˊ ㄌㄧˇ | 1/2 kilometer |
| 4 | 名不見經傳 | míngbújiàn jīngzhuàn | ㄇㄧㄥˊ ㄅㄨˊ ㄐㄧㄢˋ ㄐㄧㄥ ㄓㄨㄢˋ | unheard of; not famous |
| 5 | 曾經 | céngjīng | ㄘㄥˊ ㄐㄧㄥ | once; used to |
| 6 | 帽子 | màozi | ㄇㄠˋ ㄗ˙ | hat |
| 7 | 市場 | shìcháng | ㄕˋ ㄔㄤˊ | market |
| 8 | 運 | yùn | ㄩㄣˋ | to bring; to transport |
| 9 | 燈市 | dēngshì | ㄉㄥ ㄕˋ | lantern show |

| | | | | |
|---|---|---|---|---|
| 10 | 業務 | yèwù | ㄧㄝˋ ㄨˋ | business; profession |
| 11 | 商業中心 | shāngyèzhōngxīn | ㄕㄤ ㄧㄝˋ ㄓㄨㄥ ㄒㄧㄣ | shopping center; shop |
| 12 | 流水 | liúshuǐ | ㄌㄧㄡˊ ㄕㄨㄟˇ | flowing water |
| 13 | 一百萬 | yībǎiwàn | ㄧ ㄅㄞˇ ㄨㄢˋ | one million |
| 14 | 近代 | jìndài | ㄐㄧㄣˋ ㄉㄞˋ | modern times |
| 15 | 好處 | hǎochù | ㄏㄠˇ ㄔㄨˋ | advantages |
| 16 | 低 | dī | ㄉㄧ | low |
| 17 | 電視 | diànshì | ㄉㄧㄢˋ ㄕˋ | television |
| 18 | 方式 | fāngshì | ㄈㄤ ㄕˋ | manner; style |
| 19 | 旅遊 | lǚyóu | ㄌㄩˇ ㄧㄡˊ | travel |
| 20 | 便宜 | piányí | ㄆㄧㄢˊ ㄧˊ | cheap |
| 21 | 麥當勞 | màidāngláo | ㄇㄞˋ ㄉㄤ ㄌㄠˊ | McDonald's Restaurant |

# 第七章　王府井大街和变化中的消费生活

　　王府井¹大街是北京最有名的商业区，它从南面的长安街开始，到北面的中国美术馆²，一共大约有三华里³路那么长。大概在一千年前，这里不过是一个名不见经传⁴的小地方，后来，这里的人越来越多，据说，是因为曾经⁵有十个地方的王就住在这里，他们建了十座很漂亮的王宫，王宫也叫做王府。所以，后来人们就把这里叫做王府井。

　　从那以后，王府井就有人在做生意了，开始的时候多半是卖帽子⁶的生意。后来有人开起了简单的小店。日子久了，各种小店越来越多，最后变成了一个很大的市场⁷。慢慢地，全国各地的东西都运⁸到这里来卖。

　　到了一九〇〇年，王府井已经是北京一个很热闹的地方了。当时，王府井附近常常有灯市⁹。因为灯市很出名，所以游览的人特别多。这样，来王府井的人也就多了。人们看完灯市就到王府井来买东西。慢慢地，这里成了一个很大的商业区。二十年代的时候，许多的外国商人也在这里开始各种的业务[10]。所以，王府井许多的商店都很老了，有的是几十年，还有的是一百多年的历史了。

从五十年代开始，王府井大街有了很大的发展和变化。许多新的商业中心[11]建起来了，商店和广告到处都是。每天来到这里的人群像流水[12]一样，最多的时候差不多有一百万[13]人。

王府井的许多商店差不多都是最有名的。这里有北京烤鸭店，中国第一有名的中药房、和许许多多的老字号。现在，王府井大街是北京最古老、最有名、也是最热闹的三大商业中心之一。

但是，中国的商业发展为什么这么慢呢？中国文化有几千年的历史，而商业的发展却是在近代[14]的事。这是因为，在古时候中国文化对商业是很不重视的。不但不重视，反而认为商业对社会和人民的思想不一定有好处[15]。古时候的中国人认为，商业会使人变得自私，而太多的自私常常会使人和人之间变得非常紧张。这样，国家和社会就容易发生很多的问题。

因为这个原因，中国人几千年来的生活一直非常简单，也没有很多的变化。传统的观念告诉人们，只要有饭吃，有衣服穿和有书读，一个人的生活就是很幸福了。结果，中国社会一直发展很慢。中国人的生活一直也是很低[16]的。

只是到了最近的二十年，中国人的思想才有了很大的变化。特别是因为看到了西方社会的发展，中国人才感到商业对现代的中国社会是非常重要的。因为这个原因，政府开始接受西方国家的一些观念，重视商业在中国的发展。

近几年来，中国发生了很大的变化。人民的生活越来越好。电视[17]已经成了每个家庭生活的重要一部分。越来越多的中国家庭已经有了电话。同时，中国人对钱的观念开始有了很大的变化。以前，中国人的观念是有钱不花钱。虽然有钱，可是不把钱拿出来用。结果，生活得很辛苦，很累。现在，很多人的看法变了。人们觉得，钱是给人用的，而不是人给钱用的。应该花的钱是不能不花的。

另外，中国人花钱的方式[18]也有了变化。以前人们的钱主要是花在吃饭和穿衣服这两件事情上，很少花在其他的方面。现在，许多人开始注意花钱在教育和旅游[19]这一些方面。以前，中国人对吃饭是不随便的。吃饭一定要吃热的，要有几个菜，一个汤。现在，很多人已经接受了快餐的概念。快餐非常简单，也很便宜[20]。世界上最大的"麦当劳[21]快餐厅"就在王府井大街。

　　王府井大街的发展，是北京人生活变化的象征。现代商业文化已经成了北京人文化生活的一个重要部分。在王府井大街上，你也许可以看见北京人现代生活的明天。

## 阅读理解

1. 王府井大街是怎么来的？
2. 为什么王府井大街会成为一个商业中心？
3. 最开始王府井的名字是什么意思？
4. 王府井有多少年的历史？
5. 中国历史上的商业为什发展很慢？
6. 最近二十年来，中国的商业有什么发展和变化？
7. 中国人的消费生活有那些变化？
8. 为什么中国人现在喜欢西方的消费方式？

## 生字

| | | | |
|---|---|---|---|
| 1 | 王府井 | wángfǔjǐng | Wang Fu Jin, a shopping street in Beijing |
| 2 | 中国美术馆 | zhōngguóměishùguǎn | Chinese Gallery of Fine Arts |
| 3 | 华里 | huálǐ | 1/2 kilometer |
| 4 | 名不见经传 | míngbújiànjīngzhuàn | unheard of; not famous |
| 5 | 曾经 | céngjīng | once; used to |
| 6 | 帽子 | màozi | hat |
| 7 | 市场 | shìcháng | market |
| 8 | 运 | yùn | to bring; to transport |
| 9 | 灯市 | dēngshì | lantern show |
| 10 | 业务 | yèwù | business; profession |
| 11 | 商业中心 | shāngyèzhōngxīn | shopping center; shop |
| 12 | 流水 | liúshuǐ | flowing water |
| 13 | 一百万 | yībǎiwàn | one million |
| 14 | 近代 | jìndài | modern times |
| 15 | 好处 | hǎochù | advantages |
| 16 | 低 | dī | low |
| 17 | 电视 | diànshì | television |
| 18 | 方式 | fāngshì | manner; style |
| 19 | 旅游 | lǚyóu | travel |
| 20 | 便宜 | piányí | cheap |
| 21 | 麦当劳 | màidāngláo | McDonald's Restaurant |

# Chapter 7  Wang Fu Jing Avenue and Changing Consumerism

Wang Fu Jing Avenue is Beijing's most famous shopping district. It starts in the south at Chang An Jie (Avenue of Eternal Peace) and goes all the way to the Chinese Gallery of Fine Arts. Altogether it is about 1.5 kilometers long. Around a thousand years ago, it was no more than an unknown insignificant place. As time passed, it became more and more populated. According to legend, kings from ten different places used to live there. They built ten beautiful palaces and called the area Wang Fu (King's Residence), which is why people later called it Wang Fu Jing.

Wang Fu Jing has since become a place for commerce. In the beginning, most of the businesses were hat vendors. Later, people opened small shops, and as time went by this variety of shops developed into a large market. Slowly but surely, different products from all over the country were brought to Wang Fu Jing and sold.

In 1900, Wang Fu Jing had already become one of Beijing's lively and exciting districts. There were often lantern shows in the vicinity of Wang Fu Jing. The lantern shows became so famous that more and more tourists started going there. As a result, more people went to Wang Fu Jing as well. After viewing the lanterns, the people ended up shopping on Wang Fu Jing. Slowly but surely, the area turned into a shopping district. During the 1920s, a variety of foreign businesses opened there too. Many of the stores on Wang Fu Jing have been there for a long time, some for several decades, others for over 100 years.

In the 1950s, Wang Fu Jing went through another major transformation. Many new stores were built so there were shops and advertisements everywhere. The crowds of people who went there everyday flowed through the street like water. In business season, there were one million visitors there in a single day.

Many of the stores in Wang Fu Jing are very famous. The Beijing Duck Restaurant is located there, along with China's foremost Chinese medicine store, and many, many other Old Famous Stores. Nowadays, Wang Fu Jing is the oldest, most famous, and most lively of Beijing's three shopping centers.

Why did it take China's commerce so long to develop? Chinese culture is several thousand years old but its commerce has only recently evolved. The reason for this is that in ancient China commerce was not valued. On the contrary, it was believed that trade had a bad influence on society and its people. People used to believe that doing business would cause selfishness. Too much selfishness would create tension between people which, in turn, would cause problems to arise in the country and the society.

For that reason, the Chinese remained uncomplicated for several thousand years, with very few changes. Traditionally, the attitude was that if you had enough food to eat, enough clothes to wear and books to read, life would be very happy. As a result, Chinese society developed very slowly and the standard of living remained very low.

It has only been in the last twenty years that the Chinese way of thinking has greatly changed. Looking at western developed societies, the Chinese began to understand that commerce is very important for Chinese society today. The Chinese government started to accept some of the western concepts and paid more attention to the development of commerce in China.

China has changed a lot in recent years. People's living standards have also improved. Television has become an important part of each household and more Chinese families have telephones. The concept of money has also changed for China. In earlier times, the Chinese believed that you shouldn't spend money. Even if you had money, you didn't take it out and spend it. Life was hard and exhausting because of this. Many people now have a different outlook. People now understand that money should be used by people, people should not be owned by money. Money is meant to be used and should be spent on necessities.

The manner in which the Chinese spend their money has also changed. People used to spend their money only on food and clothes, very rarely did they use it for anything else. Now people are beginning to spend their money on education and travel. The Chinese attitude to food has also changed, it used to be quite formal. Food had to be eaten hot and there had to be several dishes, along with soup. Today, the concept of fast food has been accepted. Fast food is simple and cheap. There is even the world's biggest McDonalds on Wang Fu Jing.

The development on Wang Fu Jing Avenue is a symbol of the change occurring in people's lives in Beijing. Modern commercialism has become an important part of the people's culture. On Wang Fu Jing Avenue you can probably see the future of modern life in Beijing.

# 第八章　中小學生的學校生活

　　在北京的中小學裏，學生的生活和中國其他的地方差不多，不同的地方也許是，北京的條件要比別的地方好，北京是中國的首都，這裏可以知道從世界上各個國家和地方來的信息[1]。但是，北京中小學生的生活是很簡單的，

他們的生活就是念書、念書、再念書，這種的學生生活在全中國都是差不多的。

中小學的學生生活相當的辛苦，特別是中學的學生，中學的學生們必須在早上七點半就到學校，到學校以後，在上午的課開始以前，學生們有半個小時的時間來作準備，如：自己讀書，問老師問題，因為中國的大學不夠多，而每年高中畢業的學生卻很多，在這種情況下，高中畢業的學生裏，大約[2]只有百分之十左右的人才能考上[3]大學，所以，高中學生的升學壓力[4]很大，他們每個人都要參加全國的升學考試。考完試以後，就只有極為少數的幸運者[5]才能順利[6]的去大學唸書，其他的學生就只能找別的出路[7]了，有時他們常常一邊工作，一邊[8]繼續他們的教育。

為了能夠上大學，每個學生都非常努力[9]地學習，他們知道，如果他們不能考上大學，他們以後的工作機會將可能不會很好。雖然現在中國的變化很大，工作的機會越來越好，越來越多。可是，現在的中國還不是一個充滿機會的國家，不是每一個人都有很好的機會，所以教育是很重要的。

學生們的生活很辛苦，在學校裏，學生學習的東西很多。其中[10]以畢業的前一年，學生最忙。他們一個星期要學習六天。有些地方的學生還住在學校，他們只有在星期天[11]才能回家。他們常用背書[12]的方法來學習。背書是中國幾千年來，人們非常熟悉[13]的學習方法。中國有一句古話：如果你熟讀[14]很多的書，你也就會寫書了，熟讀其實就是背書的方法。雖然很多人熟悉這個方法，但人們也都知道，這不是一個最好的方法。

在學校裏，每一節課是四十五分鐘，每節課下課以後有十分鐘的休息，每天上午有四節課，這些課常常都是比較重要的課。中午時學校休息一個半小時[15]，許多學生都會回自己的家吃中飯[16]。這些年來，越來越多的學校開始為學生們準備中飯，在學校裏吃中飯的學生也越來越多了。

下午的時間，學生們的主要功課是在學校裏複習[17]上午學的東西，下午還有一些課是學生們喜歡的，如：學習音樂，美術和打籃球[18]等等。晚上，學生們都有家庭作業[19]必須在家裏做，老師指定[20]學生們做的家庭作業常常是很多的。有些學校，在每一次考試以後，老師都要告訴大家考試的成績。每一個人都知道誰是第一名、第二名，誰是最後一名，學生因為不喜歡自己是最後一名，所以學習會很努力。

在中國的學校裏，一班[21]大約有三十多個人，其中有一點是很特別的，就是每個班都有一名班主任[22]老師。班主任就像孩子們的父母一樣,每天都要跟學生們見面,他必須知道每一個學生的學習和生活,他常常需要找學生談話,幫助他們;也需要找學生的父母談話,告訴父母們他們的孩子在學校裏的生活,班主任的工作很多,除了這些事情以外,他還有教課的工作。因為有了班主任,學生的父母就可以放心多了,班主任常常要和學生們在一起幾年,所以他幾乎知道每個學生的事情。

學校很注意家庭對學生的影響,每一個學期,班主任老師都會去學生的家裏和家長談話,謝謝家長給學生的幫助,希望家長幫助學生學得更好。每一個學期完了的時候,學校也會舉行家長會,學校請家長們到學校,在家長會上,每個班的班主任和老師會向家長們報告,有關學生們的成績和在學校裏的表現。如果家長們知道自己孩子的學習成績不好,或者在學校裏的表現不好,就會要求自己的孩子努力學習。如果家長們知道自己的孩子學習成績很好,而且在學校的表現也很好,他們就會很高興。通常家長也是很努力的,雖然他們很忙,他們還是常常在家裏幫助孩子們完成他們的作業。

現在,很多人都覺得教育不應該只是在學校裏念書,教育一個人可以有很多的方面,很多的方法。許多的學校開始用現代的教育方法,如讓學生自己發現問題和提出問題,自己思想,同時,學校也很注意學生們的學習興趣,而不是只用背書的方法了。

學生們的課外活動[23]很多,也是很有意思的。他們經常在一起玩乒乓球[24],或者去看電影,現在越來越多的人有了電腦[25],所以學生們就在一起玩電腦。中學的學生到處都是一樣的,都喜歡玩,不太喜歡學習。在中國,中學的學生是不可以有男朋友[26]或女朋友的,交異性朋友[27]這件事,常常是一件讓父母們緊張[28],也是讓年輕人和父母之間鬧意見[29]的一件事情。

## 閱讀理解

一、北京的學校條件和中國其他地方有什麼不同?
二、為什麼中小學學生的生活不容易?
三、你贊成學生在中學階段交異性朋友嗎?
四、為什麼以前的中國人喜歡背書?
五、北京的中小學生是怎樣過他的一天的?
六、家長對學生的教育有那些影響?
七、你對中國中小學的教育的看法。

## 生字

| | | | | |
|---|---|---|---|---|
| 1 | 信息 | xìnxī | ㄒㄧㄣˋ ㄒㄧ | information; news |
| 2 | 大約 | dàyuē | ㄉㄚˋ ㄩㄝ | about; around |
| 3 | 考上 | kǎoshàng | ㄎㄠˇ ㄕㄤˋ | to pass the (college) entering exam |
| 4 | 升學壓力 | shēngxuéyālì | ㄕㄥ ㄒㄩㄝˊ ㄧㄚ ㄌㄧˋ | pressure from competition get into college |
| 5 | 幸運者 | xìngyùnzhě | ㄒㄧㄥˋ ㄩㄣˋ ㄓㄜˇ | lucky person |
| 6 | 順利 | shùnlì | ㄕㄨㄣˋ ㄌㄧˋ | smooth; without interference |
| 7 | 出路 | chūlù | ㄔㄨ ㄌㄨˋ | path |
| 8 | 一邊…一邊… | yībiān…yībiān… | ㄧ ㄅㄧㄢ … ㄧ ㄅㄧㄢ … | to do … and simultaneously do… |
| 9 | 努力 | nǔlì | ㄋㄨˇ ㄌㄧˋ | to endeavor to |
| 10 | 其中 | qízhōng | ㄑㄧˊ ㄓㄨㄥ | among |
| 11 | 星期天 | xīngqítiān | ㄒㄧㄥ ㄑㄧˊ ㄊㄧㄢ | Sunday |
| 12 | 背書 | bèishū | ㄅㄟˋ ㄕㄨ | to learn by rote |
| 13 | 熟悉 | shúxī | ㄕㄨˊ ㄒㄧ | to be familiar with |
| 14 | 熟讀 | shúdú | ㄕㄨˊ ㄉㄨˊ | to be familiar with books |
| 15 | 一個半小時 | yīgèbànxiǎoshí | ㄧ ㄍㄜˋ ㄅㄢˋ ㄒㄧㄠˇ ㄕˊ | one and a half hours |
| 16 | 中飯 | zhōngfàn | ㄓㄨㄥ ㄈㄢˋ | lunch |
| 17 | 複習 | fùxí | ㄈㄨˋ ㄒㄧˊ | to review |
| 18 | 籃球 | lánqiú | ㄌㄢˊ ㄑㄧㄡˊ | basketball |
| 19 | 家庭作業 | jiātíngzuòyè | ㄐㄧㄚ ㄊㄧㄥˊ ㄗㄨㄛˋ ㄧㄝˋ | homework |

| | | | | |
|---|---|---|---|---|
| 20 | 指定 | zhǐdìng | ㄓˇ ㄉㄧㄥˋ | assigned |
| 21 | 班 | bān | ㄅㄢ | class |
| 22 | 班主任 | bānzhǔrèn | ㄅㄢ ㄓㄨˇ ㄖㄣˋ | class advisor |
| 23 | 課外活動 | kèwàihuódòng | ㄎㄜˋ ㄨㄞˋ ㄏㄨㄛˊ ㄉㄨㄥˋ | extracurricular activities |
| 24 | 乒乓球 | pīngpāngqiú | ㄆㄧㄥ ㄆㄤ ㄑㄧㄡˊ | Ping Pong |
| 25 | 電腦 | diànnǎo | ㄉㄧㄢˋ ㄋㄠˇ | computer |
| 26 | 男朋友 | nánpéngyou | ㄋㄢˊ ㄆㄥˊ ㄧㄡ | boyfriend |
| 27 | 異性朋友 | yìxìngpéngyou | ㄧˋ ㄒㄧㄥˋ ㄆㄥˊ ㄧㄡ | friend of the opposite sex |
| 28 | 緊張 | jǐnzhāng | ㄐㄧㄣˇ ㄓㄤ | nervous |
| 29 | 鬧意見 | nàoyìjiàn | ㄋㄠˋ ㄧˋ ㄐㄧㄢˋ | difference of opinion; conflict |

# 第八章　中小学生的学校生活

　　在北京的中小学里，学生的生活和中国其他的地方差不多，不同的地方也许是，北京的条件要比别的地方好，北京是中国的首都，这里可以知道从世界上各个国家和地方来的信息[1]。但是，北京中小学生的生活是很简单的，他们的生活就是念书、念书、再念书，这种的学生生活在全中国都是差不多的。

　　中小学的学生生活相当的辛苦，特别是中学的学生，中学的学生们必须在早上七点半就到学校，到学校以后，在上午的课开始以前，学生们有半个小时的时间来作准备，如：自己读书，问老师问题，因为中国的大学不够多，而每年高中毕业的学生却很多，在这种情况下，高中毕业的学生里，大约[2]只有百分之十左右的人才能考上[3]大学，所以，高中学生的升学压力[4]很大，他们每个人都要参加全国的升学考试。考完试以后，就只有极为少数的幸运者[5]才能顺利[6]的去大学念书，其他的学生就只能找别的出路[7]了，有时他们常常一边工作，一边[8]继续他们的教育。

为了能够上大学，每个学生都非常努力[9]地学习，他们知道，如果他们不能考上大学，他们以后的工作机会将可能不会很好。虽然现在中国的变化很大，工作的机会越来越好，越来越多。可是，现在的中国还不是一个充满机会的国家，不是每一个人都有很好的机会，所以教育是很重要的。

学生们的生活很辛苦，在学校里，学生学习的东西很多。其中[10]以毕业的前一年，学生最忙。他们一个星期要学习六天。有些地方的学生还住在学校，他们只有在星期天[11]才能回家。他们常用背书[12]的方法来学习。背书是中国几千年来，人们非常熟悉[13]的学习方法。中国有一句古话：如果你熟读[14]很多的书，你也就会写书了，熟读其实就是背书的方法。虽然很多人熟悉这个方法，但人们也都知道，这不是一个最好的方法。

在学校里，每一节课是四十五分钟，每节课下课以后有十分钟的休息，每天上午有四节课，这些课常常都是比较重要的课。中午时学校休息一个半小时[15]，许多学生都会回自己的家吃中饭[16]。这些年来，越来越多的学校开始为学生们准备中饭，在学校里吃中饭的学生也越来越多了。

下午的时间，学生们的主要功课是在学校里复习[17]上午学的东西，下午还有一些课是学生们喜欢的，如：学习音乐，美术和打篮球[18]等等。晚上，学生们都有家庭作业[19]必须在家里做,老师指定[20]学生们做的家庭作业常常是很多的。有些学校,在每一次考试以后,老师都要告诉大家考试的成绩。每一个人都知道谁是第一名、第二名,谁是最后一名,学生因为不喜欢自己是最后一名,所以学习会很努力。

在中国的学校里,一班[21]大约有三十多个人,其中有一点是很特别的,就是每个班都有一名班主任[22]老师。班主任就像孩子们的父母一样,每天都要跟学生们见面,他必须知道每一个学生的学习和生活,他常常需要找学生谈话,帮助他们;也需要找学生的父母谈话,告诉父母们他们的孩子在学校里的生活,班主任的工作很多,除了这些事情以外,他还有教课的工作。因为有了班主任,学生的父母就可以放心多了,班主任常常要和学生们在一起几年,所以他几乎知道每个学生的事情。

学校很注意家庭对学生的影响,每一个学期,班主任老师都会去学生的家里和家长谈话,谢谢家长给学生的帮助,希望家长帮助学生学得更好。每一个学期完了的时候,学校也会举行家长会,学校请家长们到学校,在家长会上,每个班的班主任和老师会向家长们报告,有关学生们的成绩和在学校里的表现。如果家长们知道自己孩子的学习成绩不好,或者在学校里的表现不好,就会要求自己的孩子努力学习。如果家长们知道自己的孩子学习成绩很好,而且在学校的表现也很好,他们就会很高兴。通常家长也是很努力的，虽然他们很忙，他们还是常常在家里帮助孩子们完成他们的作业。

现在，很多人都觉得教育不应该只是在学校里念书，教育一个人可以有很多的方面，很多的方法。许多的学校开始用现代的教育方法，如让学生自己发现问题和提出问题，自己思想，同时，学校也很注意学生们的学习兴趣，而不是只用背书的方法了。

学生们的课外活动[23]很多，也是很有意思的。他们经常在一起玩乒乓球[24]，或者去看电影，现在越来越多的人有了电脑[25]，所以学生们就在一起玩电脑。中学的学生到处都是一样的，都喜欢玩，不太喜欢学习。在中国，中学的学生是不可以有男朋友[26]或女朋友的，交异性朋友[27]这件事，常常是一件让父母们紧张[28]，也是让年轻人和父母之间闹意见[29]的一件事情。

# 阅读理解

1. 北京的学校条件和中国其他地方有什么不同？
2. 为什么中小学学生的生活不容易？
3. 你赞成学生在中学阶段交异性朋友吗？
4. 为什么以前的中国人喜欢背书？
5. 北京的中小学生是怎样过他的一天的？
6. 家长对学生的教育有那些影响？
7. 你对中国中小学的教育的看法。

## 生字

| | | | |
|---|---|---|---|
| 1 | 信息 | xìnxī | information; news |
| 2 | 大约 | dàyuē | about; around |
| 3 | 考上 | kǎoshàng | to pass the (college) entering exam |
| 4 | 升学压力 | shēngxuéyālì | pressure from competition get into college |
| 5 | 幸运者 | xìngyùnzhě | lucky person |
| 6 | 顺利 | shùnlì | smooth; without interference |
| 7 | 出路 | chūlù | path |
| 8 | 一边…一边… | yībiān…yībiān… | to do … and simultaneously do… |
| 9 | 努力 | nǔlì | to endeavor to |
| 10 | 其中 | qízhōng | among |
| 11 | 星期天 | xīngqítiān | Sunday |
| 12 | 背书 | bèishū | to learn by rote |
| 13 | 熟悉 | shúxī | to be familiar with |
| 14 | 熟读 | shúdú | to be familiar with books |
| 15 | 一个半小时 | yīgèbànxiǎoshí | one and a half hours |
| 16 | 中饭 | zhōngfàn | lunch |
| 17 | 复习 | fùxí | to review |
| 18 | 篮球 | lánqiú | basketball |
| 19 | 家庭作业 | jiātíngzuòyè | homework |
| 20 | 指定 | zhǐdìng | assigned |
| 21 | 班 | bān | class |
| 22 | 班主任 | bānzhǔrèn | class advisor |
| 23 | 课外活动 | kèwàihuódòng | extracurricular activities |
| 24 | 乒乓球 | pīngpāngqiú | Ping Pong |
| 25 | 电脑 | diànnǎo | computer |
| 26 | 男朋友 | nánpéngyou | boyfriend |
| 27 | 异性朋友 | yìxìngpéngyou | friend of the opposite sex |
| 28 | 紧张 | jǐnzhāng | nervous |
| 29 | 闹意见 | nàoyìjiàn | difference of opinion; conflict |

# Chapter 8   Life in Middle and Elementary Schools

Life in Beijing's middle and elementary schools is about the same as in any middle or elementary school in China. Although people may think that the conditions are better in Beijing because it is China's capital and that one can get news from all other countries and places in the world, life for the pupils in middle and elementary schools is very simple. Their lives consists only of study, study, and more study. This life-style is about the same all over China.

Life is not easy for middle and elementary school students, especially for middle school students. The children have to be at school at 7:30 in the morning. When they get to school, before the morning lessons begin, they have half an hour to get prepared, during which time they can study or ask the teacher questions. There are not enough universities in China, but there are very many high school graduates each year. Because of this situation, among those graduating from high school, only about ten percent can go to a university. That is why there is a lot of pressure to study hard during high school. All the students need to participate in the national exams. After the exams, only a handful of lucky ones can attend university without difficulty. The other students will have to find another path. Often they end up working while continuing their education at the same time.

In order to be able to go to a university, the pupils study very diligently. They know that if they don't study at a university, their chances for a good job in the future are not great. Even though China is changing and job opportunities are getting better, it is still not a country full of opportunities. Not everyone gets a good opportunity, and that is why education is so important.

The students' lives are very hard. In school, they study too many subjects. The year before they graduate, students are the busiest. They study six days a week. Students from certain areas even live at school and only go home on Sundays. Their studying consists mainly of learning by rote. Learning by rote has been a familiar study method in China for several thousand years. There is an ancient saying in China: If you become familiar with many books, you too will be able to write books. Being familiar with books really means learning by heart. Although many people are familiar with this method, they also know that it is not the best.

Each class in school is forty-five minutes long. There is a ten-minute recess after each class. There are four classes every morning. Those are the important subjects. At noon there is an hour and a half lunch break. Many of the students go back to their own homes for lunch. In recent years, more schools have started preparing lunch in school and there are more and more students having lunch at school.

In the afternoon, the students spend most of their time in school reviewing what they learned in the morning. The students also have the kind of subjects that they enjoy in the afternoon; for example, music, art, or basketball, etc. In the evenings, the students do their homework at home. Very often the teachers assign an awful lot of homework. In school, after each exam, the teacher announces everyone's results. Everyone knows who is first, second, and last. Sometimes the students study diligently because they don't like being last.

In China, each class consists of about thirty pupils. One particularity is that each class has one teacher who acts as the class advisor. The advisor acts similarly to a parent: he or she gets together with the students everyday and has to know all about each student's study habits and his or her life. The advisor often spends time talking to the students, helping them, and even talking to their parents to let parents know all about their child's life in school. In spite of this busy task, the class advisor also teaches. The parents feel very much at ease because of the presence of the class advisor. The advisor often spends several years with the students and therefore knows all about them.

The schools also consider the family's influence on the student. Every school term the class advisor visits the students' homes. He or she talks to the head of the family and thanks him or her for helping the student and hopes that the family will help the student to study even harder. At the end of each school term, the school organizes a parent party. The parents are all invited to the school, and the advisors for each class make a report. They report on the students' grades and on their behavior. If the parents discover that their child's grades are not good or that his or her behavior was not very good, they might make their child work more diligently. If the parents find out that their child's grades and behavior have been exemplary, then they will be very happy. Many of the parents are hard working, and in spite of being very busy, they still help their children to complete their homework.

Nowadays, people realize that education needn't consist entirely of studying in school. A person's education can have many facets and many methods. Many schools are beginning to use modern educational methods; for example, students are able to make up and pose questions, and to think for themselves. Also, the schools are concerned that the students enjoy their studies and don't spend their time only learning by rote.

The students have many extra curricular activities which are a lot of fun. They play Ping Pong together or go to the movies. More and more people own computers, so the students spend time together playing on computers. Middle school students are about the same everywhere: they like to play, they don't really like to study. In China, the middle school students are not allowed to have boyfriends or girlfriends. This issue of friendship between the opposite sexes makes the parents nervous and causes conflict between the younger generation and their parents.

# 第九章　節日的北京

　　每一次節日快來的時候，北京的城市和街道都是很漂亮的。陽光、藍天、紅旗和各種顏色的旗，鮮花都一起迎接節日的來到，歡迎全國各地和從世界各個地方來的

客人。這時，人人臉上都是很高興的。節日的北京，也是很多人放假的日子，所以，人多、車多、活動也多。

以前節日的時候，北京的很多活動都是政府舉行的，政府的重要人物也會出來和人民見面、談話。

這種見面和談話叫做茶話會[2]，就是一起喝茶談話的意思，同時很多地方也有各種的表演。現在不同了，節日的活動很多都是各個公司或商店自己辦的。雖然政府也有活動，可是人們自己的活動是越來越多了，這是一個近年來的一個大變化。

中國的節日有很多，而北京因為是中國的首都，所以每一個節日都很重要。這些節日有些是文化的節日，有些是國家的節日，還有些是國際上的節日，這些節日政府都會舉行一些活動或茶話會，但並不是每一個節日都放假。

元旦[3]是每年的第一個節日，元旦又叫新年，這個節日其實是世界性[4]的節日。元旦的這一天，全國放假一天。如果還加上[5]星期天，人們就可以有兩天的休息。在北京過元旦，不像在世界其他的地方，要在一起等到半夜[6]十二點來到。中國人是在春節才算是真正的過年，春節就是中國的新年。元旦的前一天，北京並沒有什麼很特別的地方。

春節是中國最大的一個文化節日,也是北京的一個很大的節日。北京的春節有一個很大的活動,就是春節電視晚會[7],這個晚會是全中國的人民都會看,就是在世界上各地華人也都在看。春節的前一天晚上,很多非常好的表演就在電視晚會上表演。成千上萬的人就在自己的家裏,一邊吃飯,一邊看電視,一邊談自己各自的生活。然後,大家就等半夜十二點的來到,一起迎接新的一個中國年。春節的時候人們有幾天放假,可以在家裏和家人在一起。

"三八婦女節[8]"(三月八日)是一個國際婦女的節日。政府在這一天,給婦女們放假休息。因為男人們都沒有放假,所以有些男人會不高興。甚至[9]男人就希望自己在這一天是婦女,這樣可以過三八婦女節。三八婦女節對許多的婦女來說,真是一個節日,因為她們可以在這一天來作自己喜歡的事情,比如去買東西。

五月一號是國際勞動節[10]。在這天,政府也給人們放假一天休息,以前,勞動節的這一天,政府都要舉行很多的活動。因為這是一個國際的節日,所以政府也會請許多外國朋友一起參加茶話會或看表演,現在,這個節日已經不是一個很大的節日了。

六月一日是國際兒童節[11]，這是孩子們的節日，這一天，父母們都要和孩子們在一起。他們帶孩子們一起去公園，或者帶孩子們去看電影。北京的孩子們最喜歡去動物園[12]，在那裏他們可以看到各種各樣的動物。到了晚上，孩子們一定會要爸爸媽媽帶他們去吃美國快餐[13]。孩子們天天都吃中國菜，吃一次美國快餐，就能使他們覺得非常高興了。

　　十月一日是中國的國慶節，在這個節日裏全國放假兩天，以前政府在這個日子都會舉行很大的活動。現在不同了，雖然是國家的大節日，人們的活動主要還是家庭的活動。十月一日的上午，許多北京人會帶自己的小孩子去天安門廣場放[14]風箏，或者去頤和園划船[15]。也有的父母帶孩子去商店買東西。到了下午，他們會帶著孩子一起去看看爺爺[16]和奶奶[17]，和他們一起吃飯。做一點好吃的菜，和家人朋友在一起吃飯談話，在每一個節日裏，這是人們都喜歡做的事情。

　　在這些節日的裏面，北京的天氣都很好。除了元旦和春節天氣比較冷以外，其他的節日都是很暖和[18]。北京的四季都很美麗，加上節日的休息，人們的生活就很有意思的了。

# 閱讀理解

一、在北京有那些節日？哪些是文化節日？

二、什麼叫茶話會？

三、元旦和中國新年有什麼不同？

四、春節電視晚會是一個怎樣的活動？

五、三八婦女節是怎麼一回事？

六、以前的節日為什麼很多都是政府舉行的？

七、現在的節日人們主要有什麼活動？

八、孩子們過節的時候，最喜歡的是什麼活動？

## 生字

| | | | | |
|---|---|---|---|---|
| 1 | 迎接 | yíngjiē | ㄧㄥˊ ㄐㄧㄝ | to welcome; to greet |
| 2 | 茶話會 | cháhuàhuì | ㄔㄚˊ ㄏㄨㄚˋ ㄏㄨㄟˋ | tea party |
| 3 | 元旦 | yuándàn | ㄩㄢˊ ㄉㄢˋ | New Year |
| 4 | 世界性 | shìjièxìng | ㄕˋ ㄐㄧㄝˋ ㄒㄧㄥˋ | international |
| 5 | 加上 | jiāshàng | ㄐㄧㄚ ㄕㄤˋ | to add |
| 6 | 半夜 | bànyè | ㄅㄢˋ ㄧㄝˋ | midnight |
| 7 | 晚會 | wǎnhuì | ㄨㄢˇ ㄏㄨㄟˋ | party; show |
| 8 | 三八婦女節 | sānbāfùnǚjié | ㄙㄢ ㄅㄚ ㄈㄨˋ ㄋㄩˇ ㄐㄧㄝˊ | International Women' Day |
| 9 | 甚至 | shènzhì | ㄕㄣˋ ㄓˋ | even |
| 10 | 勞動節 | láodòngjié | ㄌㄠˊ ㄉㄨㄥˋ ㄐㄧㄝˊ | International Labor Day |
| 11 | 兒童節 | értóngjié | ㄦˊ ㄊㄨㄥˊ ㄐㄧㄝˊ | Children's Day |
| 12 | 動物園 | dòngwùyuán | ㄉㄨㄥˋ ㄨˋ ㄩㄢˊ | zoo |
| 13 | 快餐 | kuàicān | ㄎㄨㄞˋ ㄘㄢ | fast food restaurant |
| 14 | 放 | fàng | ㄈㄤˋ | to fly |
| 15 | 划船 | huáchuán | ㄏㄨㄚˊ ㄔㄨㄢˊ | row boat |
| 16 | 爺爺 | yéye | ㄧㄝˊ ㄧㄝ˙ | grandfather |
| 17 | 奶奶 | nǎinai | ㄋㄞˇ ㄋㄞ˙ | grandmother |
| 18 | 暖和 | nuǎnhuo | ㄋㄨㄢˇ ㄏㄨㄛ˙ | warm |

# 第九章　节日的北京

　　每一次节日快来的时候，北京的城市和街道都是很漂亮的。阳光、蓝天、红旗和各种颜色的旗，鲜花都一起迎接[1]节日的来到，欢迎全国各地和从世界各个地方来的客人。这时，人人脸上都是很高兴的。节日的北京，也是很多人放假的日子，所以，人多、车多、活动也多。

　　以前节日的时候，北京的很多活动都是政府举行的，政府的重要人物也会出来和人民见面、谈话。

　　这种见面和谈话叫做茶话会[2]，就是一起喝茶谈话的意思，同时很多地方也有各种的表演。现在不同了，节日的活动很多都是各个公司或商店自己办的。虽然政府也有活动，可是人们自己的活动是越来越多了，这是一个近年来的一个大变化。

　　中国的节日有很多，而北京因为是中国的首都，所以每一个节日都很重要。这些节日有些是文化的节日，有些是国家的节日，还有些是国际上的节日，这些节日政府都会举行一些活动或茶话会,但并不是每一个节日都放假。

元旦[3]是每年的第一个节日,元旦又叫新年,这个节日其实是世界性[4]的节日。元旦的这一天,全国放假一天。如果还加上[5]星期天,人们就可以有两天的休息。在北京过元旦,不像在世界其他的地方,要在一起等到半夜[6]十二点来到。中国人是在春节才算是真正的过年,春节就是中国的新年。元旦的前一天,北京并没有什么很特别的地方。

春节是中国最大的一个文化节日,也是北京的一个很大的节日。北京的春节有一个很大的活动,就是春节电视晚会[7],这个晚会是全中国的人民都会看,就是在世界上各地华人也都在看。春节的前一天晚上,很多非常好的表演就在电视晚会上表演。成千上万的人就在自己的家里,一边吃饭,一边看电视,一边谈自己各自的生活。然后,大家就等半夜十二点的来到,一起迎接新的一个中国年。春节的时候人们有几天放假,可以在家里和家人在一起。

"三八妇女节[8]"(三月八日)是一个国际妇女的节日。政府在这一天,给妇女们放假休息。因为男人们都没有放假,所以有些男人会不高兴。甚至[9]男人就希望自己在这一天是妇女,这样可以过三八妇女节。三八妇女节对许多的妇女来说,真是一个节日,因为她们可以在这一天来作自己喜欢的事情,比如去买东西。

五月一号是国际劳动节[10]。在这天,政府也给人们放假一天休息,以前,劳动节的这一天,政府都要举行很多的活动。因为这是一个国际的节日,所以政府也会请许多外国朋友一起参加茶话会或看表演,现在,这个节日已经不是一个很大的节日了。

六月一日是国际儿童节[11],这是孩子们的节日,这一天,父母们都要和孩子们在一起。他们带孩子们一起去公园,或者带孩子们去看电影。北京的孩子们最喜欢去动物园[12],在那里他们可以看到各种各样的动物。到了晚上,孩子们一定会要爸爸妈妈带他们去吃美国快餐[13]。孩子们天天都吃中国菜,吃一次美国快餐,就能使他们觉得非常高兴了。

十月一日是中国的国庆节,在这个节日里全国放假两天,以前政府在这个日子都会举行很大的活动。现在不同了,虽然是国家的大节日,人们的活动主要还是家庭的活动。十月一日的上午,许多北京人会带自己的小孩子去天安门广场放[14]风筝,或者去颐和园划船[15]。也有的父母带孩子去商店买东西。到了下午,他们会带着孩子一起去看看爷爷[16]和奶奶[17]，和他们一起吃饭。做一点好吃的菜，和家人朋友在一起吃饭谈话，在每一个节日里，这是人们都喜欢做的事情。

在这些节日的里面，北京的天气都很好。除了元旦和春节天气比较冷以外，其他的节日都是很暖和[18]。北京的四季都很美丽，加上节日的休息，人们的生活就很有意思的了。

## 阅读理解

1. 在北京有那些节日？哪些是文化节日？
2. 什么叫茶话会？
3. 元旦和中国新年有什么不同？
4. 春节电视晚会是一个怎样的活动？
5. 三八妇女节是怎么一回事？
6. 以前的节日为什么很多都是政府举行的？
7. 现在的节日人们主要有什么活动？
8. 孩子们过节的时候，最喜欢的是什么活动？

# 生字

1. 迎接 yíngjiē to welcome; to greet
2. 茶话会 cháhuàhuì tea party
3. 元旦 yuándàn New Year
4. 世界性 shìjièxìng international
5. 加上 jiāshàng to add
6. 半夜 bànyè midnight
7. 晚会 wǎnhuì party; show
8. 三八妇女节 sānbāfùnǚjié International Women' Day
9. 甚至 shènzhì even
10. 劳动节 láodòngjié International Labor Day
11. 儿童节 értóngjié Children's Day
12. 动物园 dòngwùyuán zoo
13. 快餐 kuàicān fast food restaurant
14. 放 fàng to fly
15. 划船 huáchuán row boat
16. 爷爷 yéye grandfather
17. 奶奶 nǎinai grandmother
18. 暖和 nuǎnhuo warm

# Chapter 9   Holidays in Beijing

When it is close to a holiday, the streets and neighborhoods of Beijing are beautifully decorated. The sunshine, the bright blue sky, the red flags and multi-colored flags, and the brightly colored flowers are all ready to greet the holiday and welcome visitors from all over China and the world. Everybody has smiles on their faces. A lot of people are off work for the holidays, which means there are many people, cars, and organized activities everywhere.

In earlier times, most of the holidays were organized by the government. Important government officials came out to see the people and talk to them.

These visits and conversations were called tea parties, which means that people drank tea together and chatted. Many places also had performances. Today it is no longer the same. Many companies and stores plan holiday activities themselves. The government still organizes things, but there are more and more activities run by the people themselves. This is a major change in recent times.

There are many holidays in China. Because Beijing is the capital, all the holidays are considered important there. Some of the holidays are cultural, others are national, and some are international. The government generally organizes some activities or tea parties for the holidays. However, people do not get time off for each of the holidays.

Yuan Dan (January 1st) is the first holiday of the year. It is also called the New Year. This is actually an international holiday. The entire country gets a day off on Yuan Dan. If a Sunday is added, then everyone has a two-day holiday. The Yuan Dan Celebration is not like the New Year Celebration in other countries where everyone waits until midnight for the new year to arrive. The Chinese do that during the Spring Festival, which is when the Chinese have their New Year's Celebration. The Spring Festival is considered China's New Year. Nothing particular happens on the eve of Yuan Dan in Beijing.

The Spring Festival is China's most important cultural holiday. It is also one of Beijing's biggest. Beijing has one very important festivity on that holiday, which is the National Celebration on TV. It is a performance which people all over China watch. Not only does all of China watch it, but Chinese from many different countries do as well. On the eve of the Spring Festival, many excellent actors perform on this television show. On this night, millions of people sit in their homes eating, watching TV, and talking about their own lives. Afterwards, everyone waits until midnight to greet the Chinese New Year. For Spring Festival, everyone has a few days off to spend at home with their families.

International Working Women's Day is an international women's holiday. On that day, the government gives all the women a day off to rest. Because the men don't have their own holiday, some of them are not happy about this holiday. Some men even wish that they were women on this day so that they could celebrate the International Women's Working day. For many women, this day is a true holiday in which they can do whatever they like. For example, they can go shopping.

International Labor Day is on May 1st. On this day as well, the government gives everyone a day to rest. The government used to organize many activities on this day. Because it is an international holiday, the government would invite foreign friends to participate in the tea parties or watch the performances. Today, this is no longer a very big holiday.

June 1st is International Children's Day, the holiday that celebrates children. On this day, all the parents want to be with their children. They go to the park with them or else they take them to see a movie. The children living in Beijing prefer going to the zoo where they can see all sorts of animals. In the evening, the children ask their parents to take them to an American fast-food restaurant. The children eat Chinese food everyday, so eating American fast-food on a special occasion makes them very happy.

Chinese National Day is on October 1st. The entire country has a two-day vacation for this holiday. The government used to organize very big celebrations on this day. This is no longer so. Although it is the National Day, people spend more time doing family activities. During the morning of October 1st, many people take their children to Tian An Men Square to fly kites or to the Summer Palace to go boating. Some parents also go shopping with their children. In the afternoon, they generally take their children to visit their grandparents and have a meal together. Cooking a good meal together and sitting with family and friends is what most people prefer doing on the holidays.

During the holidays the weather in Beijing is always very good. Except on New Year's and the Spring Festival when it is cold, the weather is generally nice and warm for the holidays. Beautiful weather during all four seasons, in addition to several days of rest during the holidays, makes life more fun.

# 第十章 北京的四合院和胡同

　　過去，人們爬上北京附近的高山，從山上往下看北京城的時候，眼前就可以看見一片綠綠的樹木和紅色的故宮樓房[1]，再看見的就是許多大大小小的四合院[2]，在那些四合院裏，住著許許多多人家[3]，原來，北京城老百姓的住

房[4]是一家一戶的平房[5]。下雨的時候，從雨裏看千千萬萬的四合院，很像一幅美麗的圖畫[6]。

　　北京的四合院分大四合院和小四合院，大四合院是以前有錢的大戶人家[7]住的，一般的老百姓，一家人只要有小四合院就夠了，小四合院是以前北京的老百姓住房的樣子。四合院多半[8]是面向[9]南邊而建的，四合院的院子裏，常常有一棵高大的樹，北京人還喜歡在院子裏種一些花草，小四合院的院子是用磚頭[10]做的，一進大門，經過院子就是一個房間，這是家中的老人住的地方，這間房間叫北屋，北屋的兩邊都有一個房間，西邊的房間是給主人住的，東邊的房間是客廳[11]。

　　四合院的建築表現了老北京人的生活，也是古老中國文化的一個代表，後來，北京的城市人口變得越來越多，原來只住一家的四合院卻住了很多家，有的四合院住了十幾家。四合院的院子裏建了許多住房或小廚房[12]，原來四合院的樣子完全沒有了。今天，政府為了保護首都的歷史文物，已經把一些四合院特別保護起來，那些不能保護的四合院很快就要被現代化的樓房所代替。

　　很多從外國來北京遊覽的客人，他們感興趣的不是那現代化的高樓和大馬路，他們最感興趣的，反而[13]是那些一條條的小胡同[14]和一座座的四合院，所以，有人把北京

的古代文化叫做 "胡同文化"和"四合院文化"這話不是沒有道理的。過去，北京千百個大大小小的四合院是背靠背[15]，面對面[16]地建成的，四合院之間走路的地方就是胡同。

北京最窄[17]的胡同是在前門[18]外的一個地方，這個胡同叫錢市胡同，胡同中間有一個地方只有四十厘米，還有些胡同不是直的，而是彎[19]的，北新橋這個地方有一個胡同，有二十多個彎，前門外也有一個胡同有十三個彎。北京的胡同裏有很多的傳說和故事，胡同好像是一部北京歷史和社會變化的百科全書[20]。

傳說很久以前，有一位外地[21]的人來北京考試，那時候，北京每年都要舉行考試，考上了的人就可以做官。所以，每年都有很多的人來北京考試，但是，這位來考試的年輕人因為沒有錢，所以是走路來北京的，到了晚上他沒有地方住，他又累又難過。這時，有一位老人走了過來，問他說：你為什麼難過呢？年輕人就把事情告訴了老人，老人說：就住在我的家吧，這位年輕人非常高興，後來才知道這條胡同裏住的十多家人以前都是做官的，他們退休[22]了以後就在這裏住下來了。年輕人因為得到這些老人的幫助，後來考試就考上了，所以這條胡同就叫老人胡同。

古時候，北京的胡同比較寬，每一條胡同都有一個名字，後來人們因為需要住房，所以又在在胡同中間的空地上建房子，這樣，許多有名的大胡同中又多出來了很多沒有名字的小胡同。有人說：有名的胡同三千六，沒名的胡同就數不清[23]了。到一九四九年，北京城裏有名字的街道有六千多條，其中胡同有一千三百多條，在北京，大大小小的胡同是北京人生活的象徵。

最近幾十年，北京的人口越來越多，變化越來越快。北京古老的胡同已經快要成為永久的歷史，在人們眼前所看到的，都已被現代的樓房所代替，這當然是非常可惜的事情。為了保護北京這個古老首都原來的樣子，許多有名的胡同已被當作歷史文物[24]保護起來了。

現在，越來越多的北京人已經開始知道，胡同是北京古老文化重要的一部分，遊覽北京胡同已經是很多的外國客人覺得非常有趣的一件事情。在北京，每天都有來自四面八方的外國朋友，坐著古老的交通工具－人力三輪車[25]，一路參觀遊覽北京的胡同文化。

你如果有機會去北京，和胡同裏普通[26]的北京人談一談，可以了解他們的實際生活，這將是一件很有意思[27]的事情，許多外國朋友們遊覽了北京的胡同後，非常高興，他們都覺得北京的胡同太美了。北京的胡同作爲北京古老文化的象徵，是非常美麗的。

## 閱讀理解

一、什麼是四合院？它是什麼樣子？
二、什麼叫胡同？爲什麼說過去的北京文化是胡同文化？
三、北京的胡同大概有多少條？
四、外國旅行參觀的人是怎樣知道胡同的？
五、當人愈來愈多的時候，北京的胡同有哪些變化？
六、古時候北方人的住房和現在有什麼不一樣？
七、老人胡同的名字是怎樣來的？

## 生字

| | | | | |
|---|---|---|---|---|
| 1 | 樓房 | lóufáng | ㄌㄡˊ ㄈㄤˊ | a building of several storeys |
| 2 | 四合院 | sìhéyuàn | ㄙˋ ㄏㄜˊ ㄩㄢˋ | a compound with houses around a courtyard |
| 3 | 人家 | rénjiā | ㄖㄣˊ ㄐㄧㄚ | household |
| 4 | 住房 | zhùfáng | ㄓㄨˋ ㄈㄤˊ | housing; lodgings |
| 5 | 平房 | píngfáng | ㄆㄧㄥˊ ㄈㄤˊ | single-storey house |
| 6 | 圖畫 | túhuà | ㄊㄨˊ ㄏㄨㄚˋ | picture; painting |

| | | | | |
|---|---|---|---|---|
| 7 | 大戶人家 | dàhùrénjiā | ㄉㄚˋ ㄏㄨˋ ㄖㄣˊ ㄐㄧㄚ | big, wealthy family |
| 8 | 多半 | duōbàn | ㄉㄨㄛ ㄅㄢˋ | most |
| 9 | 面向 | miànxiàng | ㄇㄧㄢˋ ㄒㄧㄤˋ | facing |
| 10 | 磚頭 | zhuāntóu | ㄓㄨㄢ ㄊㄡˊ | brick |
| 11 | 客廳 | kètīng | ㄎㄜˋ ㄊㄧㄥ | living room |
| 12 | 廚房 | chúfáng | ㄔㄨˊ ㄈㄤˊ | kitchen |
| 13 | 反而 | fǎnér | ㄈㄢˇ ㄦˊ | instead |
| 14 | 胡同 | hútòng | ㄏㄨˊ ㄊㄨㄥˋ | narrow alley |
| 15 | 背靠背 | bèikàobèi | ㄅㄟˋ ㄎㄠˋ ㄅㄟˋ | back to back |
| 16 | 面對面 | miànduìmiàn | ㄇㄧㄢˋ ㄉㄨㄟˋ ㄇㄧㄢˋ | facing each other |
| 17 | 最窄 | zuìzhǎi | ㄗㄨㄟˋ ㄓㄞˇ | the narrowest |
| 18 | 前門 | qiánmén | ㄑㄧㄢˊ ㄇㄣˊ | a district of Beijing |
| 19 | 彎 | wān | ㄨㄢ | winding |
| 20 | 百科全書 | bǎikēquánshū | ㄅㄞˇ ㄎㄜ ㄑㄩㄢˊ ㄕㄨ | encyclopedia |
| 21 | 外地 | wàidì | ㄨㄞˋ ㄉㄧˋ | from elsewhere; not local |
| 22 | 退休 | tuìxiū | ㄊㄨㄟˋ ㄒㄧㄡ | to retire |
| 23 | 數不清 | shǔbùqīng | ㄕㄨˇ ㄅㄨˋ ㄑㄧㄥ | uncountable |
| 24 | 歷史文物 | lìshǐwénwù | ㄌㄧˋ ㄕˇ ㄨㄣˊ ㄨˋ | historical relics |
| 25 | 三輪車 | sānlúnchē | ㄙㄢ ㄌㄨㄣˊ ㄔㄜ | lit. three-wheeled cart; man-powered pedicab |
| 26 | 普通 | pǔtōng | ㄆㄨˇ ㄊㄨㄥ | ordinary |
| 27 | 有意思 | yǒuyìsī | ㄧㄡˇ ㄧˋ ㄙ˙ | interesting |

# 第十章　北京的四合院和胡同

过去，人们爬上北京附近的高山，从山上往下看北京城的时候，眼前就可以看见一片绿绿的树木和红色的故宫楼房[1]，再看见的就是许多大大小小的四合院[2]，在那些四合院里，住着许许多多人家[3]，原来，北京城老百姓的住房[4]是一家一户的平房[5]。下雨的时候，从雨里看千千万万的四合院，很像一幅美丽的图画[6]。

北京的四合院分大四合院和小四合院，大四合院是以前有钱的大户人家[7]住的，一般的老百姓，一家人只要有小四合院就够了，小四合院是以前北京的老百姓住房的样子。四合院多半[8]是面向[9]南边而建的，四合院的院子里，常常有一棵高大的树，北京人还喜欢在院子里种一些花草，小四合院的院子是用砖头[10]做的，一进大门，经过院子就是一个房间，这是家中的老人住的地方，这间房间叫北屋，北屋的两边都有一个房间，西边的房间是给主人住的，东边的房间是客厅[11]。

四合院的建筑表现了老北京人的生活，也是古老中国文化的一个代表，后来，北京的城市人口变得越来越多，原来只住一家的四合院却住了很多家，有的四合院住了十几家。四合院的院子里建了许多住房或小厨房[12]，原来四合院的样子完全没有了。今天，政府为了保护首都的历史文物，已经把一些四合院特别保护起来，那些不能保护的四合院很快就要被现代化的楼房所代替。

很多从外国来北京游览的客人，他们感兴趣的不是那现代化的高楼和大马路，他们最感兴趣的，反而[13]是那些一条条的小胡同[14]和一座座的四合院，所以，有人把北京的古代文化叫做"胡同文化"和"四合院文化"这话不是没有道理的。过去，北京千百个大大小小的四合院是背靠背[15]，面对面[16]地建成的，四合院之间走路的地方就是胡同。

北京最窄[17]的胡同是在前门[18]外的一个地方，这个胡同叫钱市胡同，胡同中间有一个地方只有四十厘米，还有些胡同不是直的，而是弯[19]的，北新桥这个地方有一个胡同，有二十多个弯，前门外也有一个胡同有十三个弯。北京的胡同里有很多的传说和故事，胡同好像是一部北京历史和社会变化的百科全书[20]。

传说很久以前，有一位外地[21]的人来北京考试，那时候，北京每年都要举行考试，考上了的人就可以做官。所以，每年都有很多的人来北京考试，但是，这位来考试的年轻人因为没有钱，所以是走路来北京的，到了晚上他没有地方住，他又累又难过。这时，有一位老人走了过来，问他说：你为什么难过呢？年轻人就把事情告诉了老人，老人说：就住在我的家吧，这位年轻人非常高兴，后来才知道这条胡同里住的十多家人以前都是做官的，他们退休[22]了以后就在这里住下来了。年轻人因为得到这些老人的帮助，后来考试就考上了，所以这条胡同就叫老人胡同。

古时候，北京的胡同比较宽，每一条胡同都有一个名字，后来人们因为需要住房，所以又在在胡同中间的空地上建房子，这样，许多有名的大胡同中又多出来了很多没有名字的小胡同。有人说：有名的胡同三千六，没名的胡同就数不清[23]了。到一九四九年，北京城里有名字的街道有六千多条，其中胡同有一千三百多条，在北京，大大小小的胡同是北京人生活的象征。

最近几十年，北京的人口越来越多，变化越来越快。北京古老的胡同已经快要成为永久的历史，在人们眼前所看到的，都已被现代的楼房所代替，这当然是非常可惜的事情。为了保护北京这个古老首都原来的样子，许多有名的胡同已被当作历史文物[24]保护起来了。

现在，越来越多的北京人已经开始知道，胡同是北京古老文化重要的一部分，游览北京胡同已经是很多的外国客人觉得非常有趣的一件事情。在北京，每天都有来自四面八方的外国朋友，坐着古老的交通工具－人力三轮车[25]，一路参观游览北京的胡同文化。

你如果有机会去北京，和胡同里普通[26]的北京人谈一谈，可以了解他们的实际生活，这将是一件很有意思[27]的事情，许多外国朋友们游览了北京的胡同后，非常高兴，他们都觉得北京的胡同太美了。北京的胡同作为北京古老文化的象征，是非常美丽的。

## 阅读理解

1. 什么是四合院？它是什么样子？
2. 什么叫胡同？为什么说过去的北京文化是胡同文化？
3. 北京的胡同大概有多少条？
4. 外国旅行参观的人是怎样知道胡同的？
5. 当人愈来愈多的时候，北京的胡同有了哪些变化？
6. 古时候北方人的住房和现在有什么不一样？
7. 老人胡同的名字是怎样来的？

# 生字

| | | | |
|---|---|---|---|
| 1 | 楼房 | lóufáng | a building of several storeys |
| 2 | 四合院 | sìhéyuàn | a compound with houses around a courtyard |
| 3 | 人家 | rénjiā | household |
| 4 | 住房 | zhùfáng | housing; lodgings |
| 5 | 平房 | píngfáng | single-storey house |
| 6 | 图画 | túhuà | picture; painting |
| 7 | 大户人家 | dàhùrénjiā | big, wealthy family |
| 8 | 多半 | duōbàn | most |
| 9 | 面向 | miànxiàng | facing |
| 10 | 砖头 | zhuāntóu | brick |
| 11 | 客厅 | kètīng | living room |
| 12 | 厨房 | chúfáng | kitchen |
| 13 | 反而 | fǎnér | instead |
| 14 | 胡同 | hútòng | narrow alley |
| 15 | 背靠背 | bèikàobèi | back to back |
| 16 | 面对面 | miànduìmiàn | facing each other |
| 17 | 最窄 | zuìzhǎi | the narrowest |
| 18 | 前门 | qiánmén | a district of Beijing |
| 19 | 弯 | wān | winding |
| 20 | 百科全书 | bǎikēquánshū | encyclopedia |

| 21 | 外地 | wàidì | from elsewhere; not local |
| 22 | 退休 | tuìxiū | to retire |
| 23 | 数不清 | shǔbùqīng | uncountable |
| 24 | 历史文物 | lìshǐwénwù | historical relics |
| 25 | 三轮车 | sānlúnchē | lit. three-wheeled cart; man-powered pedicab |
| 26 | 普通 | pǔtōng | ordinary |
| 27 | 有意思 | yǒuyìsī | interesting |

# Chapter 10  Beijing's Courtyards and Alleys

Looking down onto Beijing from the mountains surrounding the city, one used to see a green expanse of trees and the red buildings of the Forbidden City. One could also see many large and small Si He Yuan (a compound with houses around a courtyard). Lots and lots of families used to live inside those compounds. Originally, the common people in Beijing all lived in one-story family houses. Looking at the thousands and thousands of Si He Yuan on a rainy day through the pouring rain was a beautiful sight, as pretty as a painting.

Beijing's Si He Yuan were divided into larger and smaller compounds. The large Si He Yuan were where big, wealthy families used to live. For the families of the common people, the smaller Si He Yuan were enough. All the ordinary people in Beijing used to live in the smaller compounds. That was the style of housing for the common people. Most of the compounds were built facing the south. Inside the courtyard there was usually a large tree. The residents also liked planting flowers and grass inside the courtyard. The courtyard was made of brick. As soon as you entered the main gate and passed through the courtyard, you would see a building, which was where the elderly members of the family lived. It was called the Northern House. There was a building on either side of the Northern House. The house on the western side was where the owner of the house lived. The house on the east served as a living room.

The architecture of the courtyards is a manifestation of life in earlier times, it is also a manifestation of the culture of ancient China.

Later on, the city of Beijing became too crowded. The one-family Si He Yuan now housed many families. Some of them housed more than ten families. Many little apartments or kitchens were built inside the courtyards. The original style of the Si He Yuan disappeared completely. The government has now put some of the Si He Yuan under special preservation in order to protect the capital's historical relics. The compounds which are not protected will soon be replaced by modern structures.

Many of the foreign visitors who come to Beijing are not interested in the new high rises and the wide avenues. Instead, they are most interested in all the little Hu Tong (alleys) and the many Si He Yuan. Some say that Beijing's ancient culture could be called "Alley culture" and "Si He Yuan culture." This is quite true. In the past, Beijing had hundreds of thousands of Si He Yuan all back to back, built across from each other. The narrow paths between the Si He Yuan are called Hu Tong (alleys).

The narrowest Hu Tong in Beijing are just outside of Qian Men. It is called the Qian Shi Alley. One section among those alleys is only forty centimeters wide. Also, some of the alleys are not straight, but winding. There is one Hu Tong near Bei Xin Qiao that has more than twenty curves. Outside of Qian Men there is also one with thirteen curves. There are many legends and stories about Beijing's Hu Tong. The alleys are like an encyclopedia of Beijing's history and its societal changes.

A long time ago, according to legend, a man came to Beijing to take his exam. Every year exams were held in Beijing. The people who managed to pass the exam could then secure an official position.

Many people came to Beijing every year to take the exam. However, the young man who came to take his exam didn't have any money, so he walked all the way to Beijing. He had no place to stay at night and he felt tired and sad. At that time, an old man came up to him and asked, "Why are you so sad?" The young man told him everything. The old man said, "Why don't you come and stay with me?" The young man was overjoyed and only then did he discover that the ten families living in the Hu Tong once all had official posts. When they retired, they had all moved to this Hu Tong. Because the young man had been helped by the old man and had succeeded in passing his exams, the Hu Tong is called "Old People's Alley."

In olden times, Beijing's Hu Tong were quite wide and each one had a name. Later on, more housing was needed, so more buildings were built wherever there was space in the alleys. Many of the big famous Hu Tong were turned into tiny nameless passageways. People say that there are 3,600 Hu Tong with a name and that there are uncountable nameless ones. In 1949, there were over 6,000 streets with names and over 1,300 Hu Tong. In Beijing, the many large and small alleys are the symbol of life in Beijing.

In the last decades, Beijing's population has greatly increased and the city has changed more and more. Beijing's old Hu Tong are disappearing forever and being replaced by modern buildings right in front of people's eyes. It is really a great pity. However, in order to preserve the old original style of the capital, many of the famous Hu Tong have already been made historic relics.

More people in Beijing are beginning to realize that the Hu Tong are an important part of Beijing's ancient culture. Many foreign tourists to Beijing have expressed how interesting a visit to the alleyways is. Everyday, foreign visitors come to Beijing from many different places and climb onto a man-powered pedicab, an old-fashioned means of transportation, and visit Beijing's ancient culture of the Hu Tong.

If you get a chance to go to Beijing and talk to some average Beijing residents living in the Hu Tong, you will get to know about their lives. It is an interesting thing to do. Many foreigners feel happy after visiting Beijing's Hu Tong, they think that Beijing's alleyways are truly beautiful. The Hu Tong of Beijing are a symbol of the ancient culture. They are extremely beautiful.

# 第十一章　北京的夜市和夜生活

北京人有過夜生活的習慣。每天太陽下山後,黑夜來臨¹的時候,街上的路燈²就亮起來了,這時,人們便帶著

全家，三五成群[3]地走出家們，高高興興地去各個夜市[4]。在那裏，人們開始過一個和白天完全不一樣的生活，白天是工作，晚上是休息，白天的時間是為別人，晚上的時間是為自己，這個時候，每個人的心情[5]都是非常好的。

北京最有名的夜市市場就是東華門夜市，這個地方在古時候就是一個夜市，不過，那時候人們把它叫作"鬼市[6]"。古時候的人常常在這裏賣自己家裏的東西，因為買賣經常是在半夜的時候開始，所以人們就把這個地方叫作鬼市，古時候的中國人相信[7]，鬼是只有晚上才出來的。

現在，東華門和古時候完全不一樣了，人們來到這裏主要是買東西而不是賣自己家裏的東西，而且，夜市到了半夜就關了而不是才開始，人們來這裏是為了休息和消遣[8]，白天和晚上的客人不一樣，市場也不一樣，白天這裏主要賣各式各樣[9]的衣服，晚上賣的東西卻主要是為了人們消遣，東華門的夜市主要是以各種小吃而出名的。

天黑下來的時候，東華門夜市的每一種小吃前都有很多的客人，有賣北方小吃的，也有賣南方小吃的，有的小吃是吃點心，有的小吃是喝湯，有的人賣麵[10]，有的人賣烤羊肉[11]，在這裏，你要吃什麼幾乎[12]就可以吃到什麼。

人們到東華門夜市來，主要是因為這裏非常方便，夜市的附近有很多的電影院，孩子們特別喜歡晚上來這裏，讓爸爸媽媽帶他們看電影，看完電影後，他們可以在這裏的夜市，吃各種他們喜歡的小吃，這裏還經常可以看到京劇的演出。

東華門夜市的東面就是有名的王府井大街，許多人都喜歡先來王府井大街買東西，然後再去東華門夜市看一看，東華門夜市的西邊就是故宮，騎自行車[13]只需要五、六分鐘就可以到天安門廣場，天安門廣場上也是每天晚上有很多人，許多人喜歡晚上去那兒走一走，每一天，東華門夜市都有很多的人，有時過了半夜，這裏的人還是不少。

北京的夜市主要是年輕人的世界，年輕人喜歡夜生活，夜市是他們常常要去的地方，年輕人每次和朋友們一起出去玩，不管是去跳舞[14]，還是去看電影，他們一定要去看一看附近的夜市，夜市也常常是青年見面的地方。北京的青年男人經常在夜市請自己的女朋友吃東西，在夜市裏，到處都可以看到一對對[15]的年輕人。

北京人的夜生活是很多的，也是很有趣的。不但有夜市，還有各種的消遣活動，電影、歌舞、京劇、和茶館到處都是。最近十多年來，北京建起了不少新的酒店[16]，這些酒店爲了做廣告[17]，得到更多的客人，也都在自己酒店的門前廣場上辦起了夜市。在這裏，也有很多的小吃，酒店門口還常常有廣場音樂會。

雖然在夜市裏見到的都是年輕人，老人們的夜生活也是非常有趣的。如果去街上和公園裏看看，你就會發現很多地方的老年人都三五成群在一起。他們有的談話，有的下棋[18]，還有的打牌[19]，他們在一起的活動就是他們的文化生活。老人們晚上常常在一起玩，心裏高興，生活就更有意思了。

　　還有的老年人，喜歡在一起唱京劇，很多的老年人到了晚上就找一個地方，自己唱起來，他們唱的時候，就有很多的人過來看。越多人看，這些老人們就越高興，他們也就唱得更大聲，有時，看的人也會跟著一起唱起來，北京人就是這樣喜歡自己找生活的樂趣[20]，遊覽北京的夜生活真是一件有趣的事情。


## 閱讀理解

一、什麼是夜市？什麼是夜生活？

二、東華門的夜市是怎樣來的？

三、人們在夜市裏的主要活動是什麼？

四、年輕人在夜市裏最喜最喜歡作什麼？

五、什麼是廣場音樂會？

六、老年人的夜生活有什麼活動？

七、東華門夜市附近有哪些有名的地方？

# 生字

| | | | | |
|---|---|---|---|---|
| 1 | 來臨 | láilín | ㄌㄞˊ ㄌㄧㄣˊ | to occur; to happen |
| 2 | 路燈 | lùdēng | ㄌㄨˋ ㄉㄥ | street lights |
| 3 | 三五成群 | sānwǔchéngqún | ㄙㄢ ㄨˇ ㄔㄥˊ ㄑㄩㄣˊ | in groups of threes and fours |
| 4 | 夜市 | yèshì | ㄧㄝˋ ㄕˋ | night market |
| 5 | 心情 | xīnqíng | ㄒㄧㄣ ㄑㄧㄥˊ | mood |
| 6 | 鬼市 | guǐshì | ㄍㄨㄟˇ ㄕˋ | Ghost Market |
| 7 | 相信 | xiāngxìn | ㄒㄧㄤ ㄒㄧㄣˋ | to believe |
| 8 | 消遣 | xiāoqiǎn | ㄒㄧㄠ ㄑㄧㄢˇ | diversion |
| 9 | 各式各樣 | gèshìgèyàng | ㄍㄜˋ ㄕˋ ㄍㄜˋ ㄧㄤˋ | all sorts of |
| 10 | 麵 | miàn | ㄇㄧㄢˋ | noodles |
| 11 | 羊肉 | yángròu | ㄧㄤˊ ㄖㄡˋ | mutton |
| 12 | 幾乎 | jīhū | ㄐㄧ ㄏㄨ | almost |
| 13 | 自行車 | zìxíngchē | ㄗˋ ㄒㄧㄥˊ ㄔㄜ | bicycle |
| 14 | 跳舞 | tiàowǔ | ㄊㄧㄠˋ ㄨˇ | to dance |
| 15 | 一對對 | yīduìduì | ㄧ ㄉㄨㄟˋ ㄉㄨㄟˋ | couples |
| 16 | 酒店 | jiǔdiàn | ㄐㄧㄡˇ ㄉㄧㄢˋ | restaurants |
| 17 | 做廣告 | zuòguǎnggào | ㄗㄨㄛˋ ㄍㄨㄤˇ ㄍㄠˋ | to advertise |
| 18 | 下棋 | xiàqí | ㄒㄧㄚˋ ㄑㄧˊ | to play chess |
| 19 | 打牌 | dǎpái | ㄉㄚˇ ㄆㄞˊ | to play cards |
| 20 | 樂趣 | lèqù | ㄌㄜˋ ㄑㄩˋ | pleasure |

# 第十一章 北京的夜市和夜生活

北京人有过夜生活的习惯。每天太阳下山后，黑夜来临[1]的时候，街上的路灯[2]就亮起来了，这时，人们便带着全家，三五成群[3]地走出家们，高高兴兴地去各个夜市[4]。在那里，人们开始过一个和白天完全不一样的生活，白天是工作，晚上是休息，白天的时间是为别人，晚上的时间是为自己，这个时候，每个人的心情[5]都是非常好的。

北京最有名的夜市市场就是东华门夜市，这个地方在古时候就是一个夜市，不过，那时候人们把它叫作"鬼市[6]"。古时候的人常常在这里卖自己家里的东西，因为买卖经常是在半夜的时候开始，所以人们就把这个地方叫作鬼市，古时候的中国人相信[7]，鬼是只有晚上才出来的。

现在，东华门和古时候完全不一样了，人们来到这里主要是买东西而不是卖自己家里的东西，而且，夜市到了半夜就关了而不是才开始，人们来这里是为了休息和消遣[8]，白天和晚上的客人不一样，市场也不一样，白天这里主要卖各式各样[9]的衣服,晚上卖的东西却主要是为了人们消遣,东华门的夜市主要是以各种小吃而出名的。

天黑下来的时候,东华门夜市的每一种小吃前都有很多的客人,有卖北方小吃的,也有卖南方小吃的,有的小吃是吃点心,有的小吃是喝汤,有的人卖面[10],有的人卖烤羊肉[11],在这里,你要吃什么几乎[12]就可以吃到什么。

人们到东华门夜市来,主要是因为这里非常方便,夜市的附近有很多的电影院,孩子们特别喜欢晚上来这里,让爸爸妈妈带他们看电影,看完电影后,他们可以在这里的夜市,吃各种他们喜欢的小吃,这里还经常可以看到京剧的演出。

东华门夜市的东面就是有名的王府井大街,许多人都喜欢先来王府井大街买东西,然后再去东华门夜市看一看,东华门夜市的西边就是故宫,骑自行车[13]只需要五、六分钟就可以到天安门广场,天安门广场上也是每天晚上有很多人,许多人喜欢晚上去那儿走一走,每一天,东华门夜市都有很多的人,有时过了半夜,这里的人还是不少。

北京的夜市主要是年轻人的世界,年轻人喜欢夜生活,夜市是他们常常要去的地方,年轻人每次和朋友们一起出去玩,不管是去跳舞[14],还是去看电影,他们一定要去看一看附近的夜市,夜市也常常是青年见面的地方。北京的青年男人经常在夜市请自己的女朋友吃东西，在夜市里，到处都可以看到一对对[15]的年轻人。

　　北京人的夜生活是很多的，也是很有趣的。不但有夜市，还有各种的消遣活动，电影、歌舞、京剧、和茶馆到处都是。最近十多年来，北京建起了不少新的酒店[16]，这些酒店为了做广告[17]，得到更多的客人，也都在自己酒店的门前广场上办起了夜市。在这里，也有很多的小吃，酒店门口还常常有广场音乐会。

　　虽然在夜市里见到的都是年轻人，老人们的夜生活也是非常有趣的。如果去街上和公园里看看，你就会发现很多地方的老年人都三五成群在一起。他们有的谈话，有的下棋[18]，还有的打牌[19]，他们在一起的活动就是他们的文化生活。老人们晚上常常在一起玩，心里高兴，生活就更有意思了。

　　还有的老年人，喜欢在一起唱京剧，很多的老年人到了晚上就找一个地方，自己唱起来，他们唱的时候，就有很多的人过来看。越多人看，这些老人们就越高兴，他们也就唱得更大声，有时，看的人也会跟着一起唱起来，北京人就是这样喜欢自己找生活的乐趣[20]，游览北京的夜生活真是一件有趣的事情。

## 阅读理解

1. 什么是夜市？什么是夜生活？
2. 东华门的夜市是怎样来的？
3. 人们在夜市里的主要活动是什么？
4. 年轻人在夜市里最喜最喜欢作什么？
5. 什么是广场音乐会？
6. 老年人的夜生活有什么活动？
7. 东华门夜市附近有哪些有名的地方？

## 生字

1. 来临 — láilín — to occur; to happen
2. 路灯 — lùdēng — street lights
3. 三五成群 — sānwǔchéngqún — in groups of threes and fours
4. 夜市 — yèshì — night market
5. 心情 — xīnqíng — mood
6. 鬼市 — guǐshì — Ghost Market
7. 相信 — xiāngxìn — to believe
8. 消遣 — xiāoqiǎn — diversion
9. 各式各样 — gèshìgèyàng — all sorts of
10. 面 — miàn — noodles
11. 羊肉 — yángròu — mutton
12. 几乎 — jīhū — almost
13. 自行车 — zìxíngchē — bicycle
14. 跳舞 — tiàowǔ — to dance
15. 一对对 — yīduìduì — couples
16. 酒店 — jiǔdiàn — restaurants
17. 做广告 — zuòguǎnggào — to advertise
18. 下棋 — xiàqí — to play chess
19. 打牌 — dǎpái — to play cards
20. 乐趣 — lèqù — pleasure

# Chapter 11  Beijing's Night Markets and Its Night Life

Traditionally, Beijing has a night life. Every evening after sunset when it starts getting dark, all the street lights light up. At this time in the evening, people take the whole family in groups of threes and fours and leave home to go to the night spots to have fun. People start to live a life quite different from their daytime life. In the daytime, everyone works; at night, people relax. The hours during the day are for others, the hours in the evening are for oneself. Everybody is in a good mood at night.

The most famous night market in Beijing is the Dong Hua Men night market. There used to be a night market there in ancient times as well. But in those days, people called it the Ghost Market. People used to go there to sell their own things. Because the market didn't start until midnight, the people called it the Ghost Market. In ancient times, people believed that ghosts only came out at night.

Today's Dong Hua Men is very different. People come mainly to buy things, not to sell their own belongings. What is more, the market closes at midnight, it doesn't start at midnight. The people go there for relaxation and diversion. Those who go during the day are different from the customers who go there at night. During the day, all sorts of clothes are bought; during the evening, only things for people's enjoyment are for sale. Dong Hua Men became famous for its wide variety of snacks.

When it starts to get dark, there are crowds in front of each snack booth at Dong Hua Men. They have refreshments from the north and refreshments from the south. Some snack counters sell pastries, others sell soup. Some people sell noodles, others sell Shishkebab. In this place you can eat almost anything you desire.

A lot of people come to Dong Hua Men because it is very conveniently located. There are many cinemas in the area. Children especially like going there at night, they get their parents to take them to the movies and after the movie, they go to the night market and eat all kinds of delicacies. It is also a place where one can see Beijing Opera performances.

To the east of Dong Hua Men night market is the well-known Wang Fu Jing Avenue. Many people first go shopping on Wang Fu Jing Avenue, then stroll over to Dong Hua Men for a look. To the west of Dong Hua Men is the Forbidden City, and it only takes five to six minutes to get to Tian An Men Square by bicycle. There are always many people on Tian An Men Square in the evening. People like to stroll around on the square. Everyday there are many people at the Dong Hua Men night market, and sometimes even after midnight the market is not empty.

The night markets of Beijing are really a world for the young. Young people like to go out at night, especially to the night market. When young people go out with their friends, whether it is to go dancing or see a movie, they always end up at the local night market afterwards. The night markets are places where the younger generation often gets together. Young men often invite their girlfriends to the night markets for a bite to eat. There are pairs of young people everywhere you look.

Beijing night life is abundant and a lot of fun. Besides the night markets, there are many other fun diversions. Cinemas, song and dance performances, Beijing Opera, and teahouses are everywhere. During the last ten years, many new restaurants have been built. In order to advertise their restaurants and to attract more customers, these eating and drinking establishments also organize night markets in the space right in front of their doors. There are also many snack bars in the area. The restaurants often have open concerts in front of their doors.

Although there are mainly young people at the night markets, the elderly have their own interesting night life. On the streets and in the parks one can see little groups of elderly people. Some are chatting, others are playing Chinese chess, and still others are playing cards. These mutual activities represent their culture. When the elderly spend time together and enjoy themselves, they feel happier and life becomes even better.

There are also some elderly people who enjoy singing Beijing Opera together. Many older people go out in the evening to find a spot and then they start to sing. As they sing, passersby stop to listen. The more people listen, the happier the old people are. Then they sing even louder. Sometimes the audience will join in the singing. This is how the citizens of Beijing find their personal pleasure in life. Seeing Beijing's night life is truly fascinating.

# 第十二章　自行車的王國

　　在世界上沒有別的國家像中國這樣，有這麼多的人騎[1]自行車，人們在生活的各個方面都要用自行車。大人們早上騎著自行車去工作，晚上騎著自行車回家，學生們騎著自行車去上學，周末[2]，人們騎自行車去商店

買東西，拜訪³親人和朋友，常常用的也是自行車，警察騎自行車辦理⁴公務⁵；郵局⁶的郵差⁷騎自行車給家家送信。在中國，自行車是這麼的多，差不多每家都有一輛自行車，有的家庭還有兩輛、三輛。所以，有人說中國是自行車的王國，這話一點也不錯。

在中國，人們用自行車就像美國人用汽車一樣，孩子們一長大，父母們就要教他們學習騎自行車。一個小學生能騎著自行車去上學，是一件他很高興的事，因為他不需要再走路去上學了。最重要的是，他現在可以和大人一樣，騎自行車做自己的事了。孩子們最喜歡父母送給他們的東西，就是一輛全新⁸的自行車。

一放學，孩子們就騎著自行車一起出去玩。在周末，他們也一起騎車去城市以外的地方去郊遊。男人們常常喜歡送一輛漂亮的自行車給自己的女朋友。在晚上，男女朋友一起騎著自行車去公園，或者去街上吃各種小吃，或者去聽音樂會。

在八十年代⁹以前，大多數的人都是騎自行車去工作的，政府的公務人員也是這樣。所以那時馬路上常見的就是自行車和公共汽車，其餘的就是大卡車¹⁰。八十年代以後，中國變化很大，在北京的馬路上，各種各樣的汽車越來越多了。但是，自行車還是人們的主要交通工具[11]，在主要的街道上，自行車道和汽車道是一樣的寬的，而且，在自行車道的兩邊都有很多的綠樹。夏天的時候，人們在綠樹下騎自行車，非常舒服，自行車是遊覽北京的一大風景。

很久以來，北京就是中國的首都。古時候，中國的皇帝要求北京城裏的路都必須是直的，而且，街道只可以建東西或者南北的方向，這樣，北京大部分的街道都是東西方向和南北方向的。因為北京是首都，北京的街道也建得特別的寬大，這樣，在北京的街道上非常容易認出[12]方向，騎自行車的人找路很方便，所以，騎自行車的人也就特別的多。每天早晨，北京到處都可以看見騎自行車去上班[13]的人們，這時，你會發現在馬路上自行車要比汽車多很多。在交通很忙的時候，坐在公共汽車或汽車裏的人們會很羨慕[14]在街道上騎自行車的人，因為，騎自行車又快又方便，還可以走近路和小路，同時，人們可以在回來的路上，順便[15]買東西回家。

在北京有一種特別的自行車，是三個輪子[16]的，叫三輪自行車或三輪車。在八十年代以前，三輪車主要是用來運東西，用它來代替小汽車，做很多的事情。八十年代以後，三輪車有了新的用處[17]。今天，在北京到處可以看到漂亮的三輪自行車，可是，三輪車不是運的一大包一大包的東西，而是坐著來北京遊覽的客人，三輪自行車現在成了三輪出租車[18]。

　　坐北京的三輪車出租車是很有趣的一件事情，雖然這種自行車很簡單，也不是像汽車那樣舒服。可是，坐在上面看北京的風景是一件很美的事情，騎三輪車的人大多是老北京。他們不一定是北京的老人，而是他們生在北京，知道北京的街道和北京的生活。他們對人很客氣，一邊騎車還一邊向客人介紹北京的風景，很多從外國來到北京遊覽的客人們，都喜歡花一些時間，坐三輪出租車來遊覽北京的城市風景和北京人民的生活，一路上，騎車的人和坐車的人都高高興興，遊覽北京的風景。

　　在北京，除了自行車，最常用的交通工具就是公共汽車和地鐵了。北京城裏從東到西，從南到北的每一條街道上都有公共汽車。在一些主要的街道上，公共汽車二十四小時都有，所以，坐公共汽車也是很方便的。現在許多北京人，常常是騎自行車同時又坐公共汽車，他們先騎自行車到自己家附近的公共汽車站，把自行車停在一個地方，然後再坐公共汽車去他們要去的地方。

　　除了公共汽車，地鐵也是北京人最常用的交通工具。北京的地鐵有兩條，一條是從東到西的地鐵，另一條是環繞北京城的地鐵，北京人很喜歡坐地鐵。在地鐵站裏，人們可以買到各種的書報[19]和雜誌[20]，也可以買到快餐和喝的東西。在地鐵裏，冬天不冷，夏天不熱，不怕風也不怕雨，等車的時候又可以看書或者看報紙，所以，北京人很喜歡坐地鐵去辦事情。每一個地鐵站都有停自行車的地方，人們經常是騎自行車到地鐵站，然後再坐地鐵去上班或辦事情。

北京人經常用的另一種交通工具是出租汽車，早在一九一三年，北京的街上就有出租汽車了，到了一九二九年，北京的出租車有二百多輛。不過，當時只有有錢人才坐出租車，一般老百姓連飯都吃不飽，當然就不可能坐出租車了。直到八十年代，因為遊覽北京的人越來越多，出租汽車這一行業[21]才開始發展起來，後來，政府也讓私人開出租汽車公司。現在，坐出租汽車的人越來越多，同時，北京出租車的數量也越來越多，據統計[22]，北京現有出租車六萬多輛，北京每天坐出租汽車人比坐地鐵的人還要多。雖然出租汽車、公共汽車、地鐵是今天北京城市交通的三大行業，人們在生活中用得最多的還是自己的自行車。

## 閱讀理解

一、為什麼說中國是自行車的王國？

二、請猜猜中國有多少輛自行車？

三、學生會騎自行車為什麼很重要？

四、為什麼自行車是遊覽北京的一大風景？

五、什麼是三輪出租車？

六、北京主要的交通工具有那些？

七、北京現在的交通有什麼變化？

# 生字

| | | | | |
|---|---|---|---|---|
| 1 | 騎 | qí | ㄑㄧˊ | to ride (a bicycle) |
| 2 | 周末 | zhōumò | ㄓㄡ ㄇㄛˋ | the weekend |
| 3 | 拜訪 | bàifǎng | ㄅㄞˋ ㄈㄤˇ | to visit |
| 4 | 辦理 | bànlǐ | ㄅㄢˋ ㄌㄧˇ | to handle |
| 5 | 公務 | gōngwù | ㄍㄨㄥ ㄨˋ | public service |
| 6 | 郵局 | yóujú | ㄧㄡˊ ㄐㄩˊ | post office |
| 7 | 郵差 | yóuchāi | ㄧㄡˊ ㄔㄞ | postal worker |
| 8 | 全新 | quánxīn | ㄑㄩㄢˊ ㄒㄧㄣ | brand-new |
| 9 | 八十年代 | bāshíniándài | ㄅㄚ ㄕˊ ㄋㄧㄢˊ ㄉㄞˋ | the 1980s |
| 10 | 卡車 | kǎchē | ㄎㄚˇ ㄔㄜ | trucks |
| 11 | 交通工具 | jiāotōnggōngjù | ㄐㄧㄠ ㄊㄨㄥ ㄍㄨㄥ ㄐㄩˋ | means of transportation |
| 12 | 認出 | rènchū | ㄖㄣˋ ㄔㄨ | recognize |
| 13 | 上班 | shàngbān | ㄕㄤˋ ㄅㄢ | go to work |
| 14 | 羨慕 | xiànmù | ㄒㄧㄢˋ ㄇㄨˋ | to envy |
| 15 | 順便 | shùnbiàn | ㄕㄨㄣˋ ㄅㄧㄢˋ | along the way |
| 16 | 輪子 | lúnzi | ㄌㄨㄣˊ ㄗ˙ | wheel |
| 17 | 用處 | yòngchù | ㄩㄥˋ ㄔㄨˋ | use; purpose |
| 18 | 出租車 | chūzūchē | ㄔㄨ ㄗㄨ ㄔㄜ | taxi |
| 19 | 書報 | shūbào | ㄕㄨ ㄅㄠˋ | books and newspapers |
| 20 | 雜誌 | zázhì | ㄗㄚˊ ㄓˋ | magazine |
| 21 | 行業 | hángyè | ㄏㄤˊ ㄧㄝˋ | profession |
| 22 | 據統計 | jùtǒngjì | ㄐㄩˋ ㄊㄨㄥˇ ㄐㄧˋ | according to statistics |

# 第十二章　自行车的王国

在世界上没有别的国家像中国这样,有这么多的人骑[1]自行车,人们在生活的各个方面都要用自行车。大人们早上骑着自行车去工作,晚上骑着自行车回家,学生们骑着自行车去上学,周末[2],人们骑自行车去商店买东西,拜访[3]亲人和朋友,常常用的也是自行车,警察骑自行车办理[4]公务[5];邮局[6]的邮差[7]骑自行车给家家送信。在中国,自行车是这么的多,差不多每家都有一辆自行车,有的家庭还有两辆、三辆。所以,有人说中国是自行车的王国,这话一点也不错。

在中国,人们用自行车就像美国人用汽车一样,孩子们一长大,父母们就要教他们学习骑自行车。一个小学生能骑着自行车去上学,是一件他很高兴的事,因为他不需要再走路去上学了。最重要的是,他现在可以和大人一样,骑自行车做自己的事了。孩子们最喜欢父母送给他们的东西,就是一辆全新[8]的自行车。

一放学，孩子们就骑着自行车一起出去玩。在周末，他们也一起骑车去城市以外的地方去郊游。男人们常常喜欢送一辆漂亮的自行车给自己的女朋友。在晚上，男女朋友一起骑着自行车去公园，或者去街上吃各种小吃，或者去听音乐会。

在八十年代[9]以前，大多数的人都是骑自行车去工作的，政府的公务人员也是这样。所以那时马路上常见的就是自行车和公共汽车，其余的就是大卡车[10]。八十年代以后，中国变化很大，在北京的马路上，各种各样的汽车越来越多了。但是，自行车还是人们的主要交通工具[11]，在主要的街道上，自行车道和汽车道是一样的宽的，而且，在自行车道的两边都有很多的绿树。夏天的时候，人们在绿树下骑自行车，非常舒服，自行车是游览北京的一大风景。

很久以来，北京就是中国的首都。古时候，中国的皇帝要求北京城里的路都必须是直的，而且，街道只可以建东西或者南北的方向，这样，北京大部分的街道都是东西方向和南北方向的。因为北京是首都，北京的街道也建得特别的宽大，这样，在北京的街道上非常容易认出[12]方向，骑自行车的人找路很方便，所以，骑自行车的人也就特别的多。每天早晨，北京到处都可以看见骑自行车去上班[13]的人们，这时，你会发现在马路上自行车要比汽车多很多。在交通很忙的时候，坐在公共汽车或汽车里的人们会很羡慕[14]在街道上骑自行车的人，因为，骑自行车又快又方便，还可以走近路和小路，同时，人们可以在回来的路上，顺便[15]买东西回家。

在北京有一种特别的自行车，是三个轮子[16]的，叫三轮自行车或三轮车。在八十年代以前，三轮车主要是用来运东西，用它来代替小汽车，做很多的事情。八十年代以后，三轮车有了新的用处[17]。今天，在北京到处可以看到漂亮的三轮自行车，可是，三轮车不是运的一大包一大包的东西，而是坐着来北京游览的客人，三轮自行车现在成了三轮出租车[18]。

坐北京的三轮车出租车是很有趣的一件事情，虽然这种自行车很简单，也不是像汽车那样舒服。可是，坐在上面看北京的风景是一件很美的事情，骑三轮车的人大多是老北京。他们不一定是北京的老人，而是他们生在北京，知道北京的街道和北京的生活。他们对人很客气，一边骑车还一边向客人介绍北京的风景，很多从外国来到北京游览的客人们，都喜欢花一些时间，坐三轮出租车来游览北京的城市风景和北京人民的生活，一路上，骑车的人和坐车的人都高高兴兴，游览北京的风景。

在北京，除了自行车，最常用的交通工具就是公共汽车和地铁了。北京城里从东到西，从南到北的每一条街道上都有公共汽车。在一些主要的街道上，公共汽车二十四小时都有，所以，坐公共汽车也是很方便的。现在许多北京人，常常是骑自行车同时又坐公共汽车，他们先骑自行车到自己家附近的公共汽车站，把自行车停在一个地方，然后再坐公共汽车去他们要去的地方。

　　除了公共汽车，地铁也是北京人最常用的交通工具。北京的地铁有两条，一条是从东到西的地铁，另一条是环绕北京城的地铁，北京人很喜欢坐地铁。在地铁站里，人们可以买到各种的书报[19]和杂志[20]，也可以买到快餐和喝的东西。在地铁里，冬天不冷，夏天不热，不怕风也不怕雨，等车的时候又可以看书或者看报纸，所以，北京人很喜欢坐地铁去办事情。每一个地铁站都有停自行车的地方，人们经常是骑自行车到地铁站，然后再坐地铁去上班或办事情。

　　北京人经常用的另一种交通工具是出租汽车，早在一九一三年，北京的街上就有出租汽车了，到了一九二九年，北京的出租车有二百多辆。不过，当时只有有钱人才坐出租车，一般老百姓连饭都吃不饱，当然就不可能坐出租车了。直到八十年代，因为游览北京的人越来越多，出租汽车这一行业[21]才开始发展起来，后来，政府也让私人开出租汽车公司。现在，坐出租汽车的人越来越多，同时，北京出租车的数量也越来越多，据统计[22]，北京现有出租车六万多辆，北京每天坐出租汽车人比坐地铁的人还要多。虽然出租汽车、公共汽车、地铁是今天北京城市交通的三大行业，人们在生活中用得最多的还是自己的自行车。

## 阅读理解

1. 为什么说中国是自行车的王国？
2. 请猜猜中国有多少辆自行车？
3. 学生会骑自行车为什么很重要？
4. 为什么自行车是游览北京的一大风景？
5. 什么是三轮出租车？
6. 北京主要的交通工具有那些？
7. 北京现在的交通有什么变化？

# 生字

| | | | |
|---|---|---|---|
| 1 | 骑 | qí | to ride (a bicycle) |
| 2 | 周末 | zhōumò | the weekend |
| 3 | 拜访 | bàifǎng | to visit |
| 4 | 办理 | bànlǐ | to handle |
| 5 | 公务 | gōngwù | public service |
| 6 | 邮局 | yóujú | post office |
| 7 | 邮差 | yóuchāi | postal worker |
| 8 | 全新 | quánxīn | brand-new |
| 9 | 八十年代 | bāshíniándài | the 1980s |
| 10 | 卡车 | kǎchē | trucks |
| 11 | 交通工具 | jiāotōnggōngjù | means of transportation |
| 12 | 认出 | rènchū | recognize |
| 13 | 上班 | shàngbān | go to work |
| 14 | 羡慕 | xiànmù | to envy |
| 15 | 顺便 | shùnbiàn | along the way |
| 16 | 轮子 | lúnzi | wheel |
| 17 | 用处 | yòngchù | use; purpose |
| 18 | 出租车 | chūzūchē | taxi |
| 19 | 书报 | shūbào | books and newspapers |
| 20 | 杂志 | zázhì | magazine |
| 21 | 行业 | hángyè | profession |
| 22 | 据统计 | jùtǒngjì | according to statistics |

# Chapter 12  The Kingdom of Bicycles

There is no other country in the world where so many people ride bicycles. People use bicycles in almost every sector of life. The adults ride their bicycles to work in the morning, and come home by bicycle in the evening. Students go to school by bicycle. On the weekends, people go to the shops by bicycle. To visit relatives and friends, people use bicycles. The police use bicycles while doing their public service, the postal workers use bicycles when delivering mail to the homes. There are so many bicycles in China that almost each family has one bicycle. There are some families that have two, or even three. This is why some people say that China is the Kingdom of Bicycles. That is quite a true statement.

In China, people use bicycles the way Americans use cars. As children grow up, their parents teach them how to ride a bicycle. If an elementary student is able to ride his bicycle to school, he will feel extremely happy because he doesn't have to walk to school anymore. The best part of riding a bicycle for a child is that he can be like a grown-up and do whatever he likes. What children like best of all is to receive a brand-new bicycle from their parents.

As soon as class is over, the children get on their bikes and go somewhere to have fun. On the weekends, they can ride their bicycles on an outing outside of the city. Young men like to give their girlfriends a beautiful new bicycle as a present. In the evenings, the couples ride their bicycles to the park or to eat some snacks along the streets, or they may go to a concert hall.

Before the 1980s, everybody went to work by bicycle, even the government officials. In those days, all one could see on the streets were bicycles and trolley buses. Big trucks were also on the streets. After the 1980s, there were many changes in China. The streets of Beijing were filled more and more with different kinds of cars. However, the bicycle is still China's most important means of transportation. On the main streets, the bicycle lanes and the car lanes are equally wide. There are trees on either side of the bicycle lanes. It is nice and cool to ride under the trees in the summer. The bicycles are one of the major sights of Beijing.

Beijing has been the capital of China for a very long time. In ancient times, the emperor required all the streets in Beijing to be straight. The streets were only allowed to be built in the east-west or north-south direction. Most of the streets in Beijing run either east-west or north-south. Because Beijing is the capital, the streets were also built especially wide. It is very easy to find one's way along the streets of Beijing and it is convenient for the cyclists. For this reason, many people ride bicycles in Beijing. Early in the morning, one can see people riding to work everywhere. In fact, there are many more bicycles than cars on the street at that time. When the traffic is the busiest, the people sitting in buses or cars may envy those riding bicycles on the streets. Bicycles are fast and convenient, they can take shortcuts and go down the narrow side streets. One can also stop to buy things on the way home.

In Beijing, there is a particular bicycle which has three wheels. It is called the three-wheeled bicycle or pedicab. Before the 1980s, the pedicab was mainly used for transporting goods, it was used instead of the car, and had many functions. After the 1980s, the pedicab had a new purpose. Now there are beautiful new pedicabs everywhere in Beijing. They no longer transport big bags of things, instead they serve to take tourists around the city. The three-wheeled bicycle has become a three-wheeled taxi!

It is a lot of fun to ride in the three-wheeled taxis. Although it is not fancy and not as comfortable as a car, it is still wonderful to see the sights of Beijing from a pedicab. The drivers are mainly from old Beijing. They are not old people from Beijing, but rather they live in Beijing and they know the streets and life of Beijing. They are very polite to people. While driving the pedicab, they explain Beijing's sights to their customers. Many foreign tourists who come to see Beijing enjoy spending a little time sitting in a pedicab and admiring the city sights and getting to know the people's lives. The driver and the passengers are happy sightseeing all along the roads of Beijing.

The other most frequently used means of transportation in Beijing are the buses and the subway. Buses run along all the streets of Beijing, east and west, north and south. On some of the major streets, the buses run twenty-four-hours-a-day. It is therefore very convenient to take the bus. Nowadays, many of the residents of Beijing ride bicycles as well as the bus. First they ride their bicycles to the bus stop nearest to their home, then they park their bicycle somewhere and take the bus to wherever they are going.

Aside from the bus, the subway is the most frequently used means of transportation in Beijing. There are two subway lines in Beijing. One runs the east-west route and the other encircles the city. The residents of Beijing like taking the subway. They can buy books and newspapers and magazines in the subway station. Fast food and drinks are also available. Inside the subway it is neither cold in winter nor hot in summer, passengers needn't fear wind or rain. While waiting for the subway, they can read a book or the newspaper. That is why the people of Beijing really like taking the subway to the office. There is a place to park bicycles at every subway station. People often ride their bicycles to the subway station and then take the subway to work or to the office.

The people of Beijing also use taxis as another means of transportation. Even in 1913 there were taxis on the streets of Beijing. In 1929, there were more than 200 taxis in Beijing. However, only wealthy people took taxis. The common people didn't even have enough food to eat and could not afford to take taxis. It was not until the 1980s when more and more tourists came to Beijing that taxi-driving started to develop as a profession. Later on, the government also permitted privately-owned taxi companies to set up business. Now there are more and more taxi drivers. The number of taxis has also increased. According to the statistics, Beijing now has over 60,000 taxis. There are more people in Beijing taking taxis daily than there are people taking the subway. Although taxis, buses, and the subway are Beijing's three major means of transportation, what people use most in their lives is still their very own bicycle.

# 第十三章　周末與郊遊

　　古時候，中國人的生活習慣和西方人有很大的不同。因為那時候的中國人大多是農民，農民的生活是不可以用七天一周的方式，農民忙的時候很忙，沒有事的時候才可以休息。七天一周的生活方式，是從西方介紹到中國來的，所以工作六天，休息一天是中國人從西方學來的。而且，這種方式只有在城市工作的人，或是給政府工作的人才有的。

　　一九九四年前，中國的城市人民和公務人員都是一周工作六天，星期天休息。這樣，人們從星期一到星期六很少有自己的時間了，他們很難有時間去買東西，或者做自己家裏的事情，星期天對許多人來說就是買東西的日子，所以，星期天去商店裏的人是最多的。除了買東西，人們還用來做許多的事情，比如：收拾房子，洗衣服[1]和處理種種的私人事情，所以，其實人們不能在星期天真正得到休息。只是在比較大的節日，如春節、五一節和國慶節，人們才會和全家一起出去玩，因為第二天有時間休息，大的節日常常會有二天的休息。

　　從一九九四年開始，中國開始接受一周工作五天的生活方式，在周末休息兩天，剛剛開始的時候，人們還不習慣。因為突然在周末多了一天的休息時間，許多人不知道應該怎麼辦[2]。不過，很快人們就變得非常喜歡這樣的工作和生活方式了，現在的北京人在周末，有很多的活動，人們可以辦自己的事情，也可以和朋友一起出去玩。還可以自己燒一些好吃的菜，高高興興地吃一下，什麼事也不想做的時候，就可以在家裏休息。

周末的時間多了，人們就會一家一家地出去郊遊，用這個時間全家在一起談話，休息和過家庭生活。很多的家庭喜歡去香山[3]玩，香山是在北京郊外的一座山，這座山很高很大，十分美麗。站在香山上可以看見很遠的地方，也可以看見北京城和其他的風景，如頤和園的昆明湖。秋天的時候，香山的紅葉[4]最好看，很多人都要在秋天來看出名的香山紅葉，古時候，皇帝也常常來遊覽香山呢！

　　也有些家庭會去天壇公園玩，天壇就是一個大台子[5]的意思，古時候的皇帝用壇來做拜天地，不同的壇用來做不同的儀式。皇帝在北京有許多的壇，天壇在北京的南面，地壇在北京的北面，還有日壇和月壇。天壇是用來拜天的，地壇是用來拜地的。每年開始的時候，皇帝都要去天壇舉行拜天的儀式。皇帝拜天，是希望上天[6]在新的一年，給他的國家有好的福氣，也給他的人民幸福的生活。

　　古時候，皇帝認爲自然的世界有很大的能力，它對一個國家有特別大的影響。中國的皇帝還認爲天上有一位神，皇帝是這位神的兒子，所以替國家舉行拜天的儀式只能由皇帝來做。在天壇裏，皇帝拜天的台子是建在一個很高的塔[7]，因爲是要拜天，所以一定要離天近一些。皇帝在地壇拜地，是希望土地有好的收成[8]。皇帝還要拜太陽和月亮，希望新的一年裏有好的天氣，不要有地震[9]。

在北京的東邊，有一個地方叫"東便門"，在東便門那裏，有一個古代觀看天氣和地震的地方。古時候，有一個科學家發明了一個儀器[10]，可以知道天氣的變化，它還可以知道會不會有地震發生。許多父母常常喜歡把孩子們帶到這裏，讓他們知道和學習中國古代的科學歷史。

最近幾年，人們過周末的方式又有了新的變化。過去，人們在周末主要是去街上買東西，或者去看看商店裏有什麼新的東西。所以，一到周末，街上的人很多。有的時候，人太多了，公共汽車不能坐，有些地方連人也不能走。可是，現在許多北京人過周末，不再常去北京有名的地方看風景了。他們而是去郊外遊覽，人們叫郊遊。

現在，去北京有名的地方遊覽的人主要是外地人和外國人。他們沒有看過北京，沒有看過像故宮、長城和天安門這樣的地方。而這些地方北京人都去過了，現在北京人更喜歡去的地方，是大家不常去的地方，有些時候，北京人喜歡去郊外[11]人少或者沒有人地方，這些地方很安靜，也很美麗，不過，這種美麗和北京的美麗不一樣。北京的美麗是首都的美，郊外的美麗是自然的美，有的時候，人們晚上還在郊外過夜[12]呢！

當然，過周末一定不能沒有[13]好吃的，中國人對吃飯從來不隨便。這也是為什麼常常聽人說，中國的文化是"吃的文化[14]"，比方說，中國人跟朋友在一起見面，吃飯可能是最重要的一個活動，如果沒有吃飯，可能見面就少了很多意思。所以，過去的周末，人們常常在家裏，做一些好吃的菜。這樣，請朋友來一起喝酒，談天，高高興興地過一個周末。可是，現在不一樣了，北京人的生活一天天地好起來，人們不需要在家裏花時間做菜了。現在的生活都很方便，所以北京人常常和朋友一起到飯店裏吃飯，這樣，請客就更容易了，北京人的周末也變得越來越有趣了。

## 閱讀理解

一、談談二、三件事，說明中國人的生活習慣和西方有什麼不同。
二、中國現在的工作休息方式有哪些變化的？
三、一九九四年以前，人們的工作休息方式是怎樣？
四、北京人周末的時候常去什麼地方？
五、天壇和地壇在古時候是作什麼用的？

# 生字

| | | | | |
|---|---|---|---|---|
| 1 | 洗衣服 | xǐyīfu | ㄒㄧˇ ㄧ ㄈㄨˊ | to do the laundry |
| 2 | 怎麼辦 | zěmobàn | ㄗㄜˇ ㄇㄛ· ㄅㄢˋ | what to do |
| 3 | 香山 | xiāngshān | ㄒㄧㄤ ㄕㄢ | Fragrant Mountain (in Beijing) |
| 4 | 紅葉 | hóngyè | ㄏㄨㄥˊ ㄧㄝˋ | red autumn leaves |
| 5 | 台子 | táizi | ㄊㄞˊ ㄗ· | platform |
| 6 | 上天 | shàngtiān | ㄕㄤˋ ㄊㄧㄢ | heaven; God |
| 7 | 塔 | tǎ | ㄊㄚˇ | pagoda |
| 8 | 收成 | shōuchéng | ㄕㄡ ㄔㄥˊ | harvest |
| 9 | 地震 | dìzhèn | ㄉㄧˋ ㄓㄣˋ | earthquake |
| 10 | 儀器 | yíqì | ㄧˊ ㄑㄧˋ | apparatus |
| 11 | 郊外 | jiāowài | ㄐㄧㄠ ㄨㄞˋ | the outskirts |
| 12 | 過夜 | guòyè | ㄍㄨㄛˋ ㄧㄝˋ | to spend the night |
| 13 | 不能沒有 | bùnéngméiyǒu | ㄅㄨˋ ㄋㄥˊ ㄇㄟˊ ㄧㄡˇ | can't ignore |
| 14 | 吃的文化 | chīdewénhuà | ㄔ ㄉㄜ· ㄨㄣˊ ㄏㄨㄚˋ | food culture |

# 第十三章　周末与郊游

古时候,中国人的生活习惯和西方人有很大的不同。因为那时候的中国人大多是农民,农民的生活是不可以用七天一周的方式,农民忙的时候很忙,没有事的时候才可以休息。七天一周的生活方式,是从西方介绍到中国来的,所以工作六天,休息一天是中国人从西方学来的。而且,这种方式只有在城市工作的人,或是给政府工作的人才有的。

一九九四年前,中国的城市人民和公务人员都是一周工作六天,星期天休息。这样,人们从星期一到星期六很少有自己的时间了,他们很难有时间去买东西,或者做自己家里的事情,星期天对许多人来说就是买东西的日子,所以,星期天去商店里的人是最多的。除了买东西,人们还用来做许多的事情,比如:收拾房子,洗衣服¹和处理种种的私人事情,所以,其实人们不能在星期天真正得到休息。只是在比较大的节日,如春节、五一节和国庆节，人们才会和全家一起出去玩，因为第二天有时间休息，大的节日常常会有二天的休息。

从一九九四年开始，中国开始接受一周工作五天的生活方式，在周末休息两天，刚刚开始的时候，人们还不习惯。因为突然在周末多了一天的休息时间，许多人不知道应该怎么办[2]。不过，很快人们就变得非常喜欢这样的工作和生活方式了，现在的北京人在周末，有很多的活动，人们可以办自己的事情，也可以和朋友一起出去玩。还可以自己烧一些好吃的菜，高高兴兴地吃一下，什么事也不想做的时候，就可以在家里休息。

周末的时间多了，人们就会一家一家地出去郊游，用这个时间全家在一起谈话，休息和过家庭生活。很多的家庭喜欢去香山[3]玩，香山是在北京郊外的一座山，这座山很高很大，十分美丽。站在香山上可以看见很远的地方，也可以看见北京城和其他的风景，如颐和园的昆明湖。秋天的时候，香山的红叶[4]最好看，很多人都要在秋天来看出名的香山红叶，古时候，皇帝也常常来游览香山呢！

也有些家庭会去天坛公园玩，天坛就是一个大台子[5]的意思，古时候的皇帝用坛来做拜天地，不同的坛用来做不同的仪式。皇帝在北京有许多的坛，天坛在北京的南面，地坛在北京的北面，还有日坛和月坛。天坛是用来拜天的，地坛是用来拜地的。每年开始的时候，皇帝都要去天坛举行拜天的仪式。皇帝拜天，是希望上天[6]在新的一年，给他的国家有好的福气，也给他的人民幸福的生活。

古时候，皇帝认为自然的世界有很大的能力，它对一个国家有特别大的影响。中国的皇帝还认为天上有一位神，皇帝是这位神的儿子，所以替国家举行拜天的仪式只能由皇帝来做。在天坛里，皇帝拜天的台子是建在一个很高的塔[7]，因为是要拜天，所以一定要离天近一些。皇帝在地坛拜地，是希望土地有好的收成[8]。皇帝还要拜太阳和月亮，希望新的一年里有好的天气，不要有地震[9]。

在北京的东边，有一个地方叫"东便门"，在东便门那里，有一个古代观看天气和地震的地方。古时候，有一个科学家发明了一个仪器[10]，可以知道天气的变化，它还可以知道会不会有地震发生。许多父母常常喜欢把孩子们带到这里，让他们知道和学习中国古代的科学历史。

最近几年，人们过周末的方式又有了新的变化。过去，人们在周末主要是去街上买东西，或者去看看商店里有什么新的东西。所以，一到周末，街上的人很多。有的时候，人太多了，公共汽车不能坐，有些地方连人也不能走。可是，现在许多北京人过周末，不再常去北京有名的地方看风景了。他们而是去郊外游览，人们叫郊游。

现在，去北京有名的地方游览的人主要是外地人和外国人。他们没有看过北京，没有看过像故宫、长城和天安门这样的地方。而这些地方北京人都去过了，现在北京人更喜欢去的地方，是大家不常去的地方，有些时候，北京人喜欢去郊外[11]人少或者没有人地方，这些地方很安静，也很美丽，不过，这种美丽和北京的美丽不一样。北京的美丽是首都的美，郊外的美丽是自然的美，有的时候，人们晚上还在郊外过夜[12]呢！

当然，过周末一定不能没有[13]好吃的，中国人对吃饭从来不随便。这也是为什么常常听人说，中国的文化是"吃的文化[14]"，比方说，中国人跟朋友在一起见面，吃饭可能是最重要的一个活动，如果没有吃饭，可能见面就少了很多意思。所以，过去的周末，人们常常在家里，做一些好吃的菜。这样，请朋友来一起喝酒，谈天，高高兴兴地过一个周末。可是，现在不一样了，北京人的生活一天天地好起来，人们不需要在家里花时间做菜了。现在的生活都很方便，所以北京人常常和朋友一起到饭店里吃饭，这样，请客就更容易了，北京人的周末也变得越来越有趣了。

## 阅读理解

1. 谈谈二、三件事，说明中国人的生活习惯和西方有什么不同。
2. 中国现在的工作休息方式有哪些变化的？
3. 一九九四年以前，人们的工作休息方式是怎样？
4. 北京人周末的时候常去什么地方？
5. 天坛和地坛在古时候是作什么用的？

## 生字

| | | | |
|---|---|---|---|
| 1 | 洗衣服 | xǐyīfu | to do the laundry |
| 2 | 怎么办 | zěmobàn | what to do |
| 3 | 香山 | xiāngshān | Fragrant Mountain (in Beijing) |
| 4 | 红叶 | hóngyè | red autumn leaves |
| 5 | 台子 | táizi | platform |
| 6 | 上天 | shàngtiān | heaven; God |
| 7 | 塔 | tǎ | pagoda |
| 8 | 收成 | shōuchéng | harvest |
| 9 | 地震 | dìzhèn | earthquake |
| 10 | 仪器 | yíqì | apparatus |
| 11 | 郊外 | jiāowài | the outskirts |
| 12 | 过夜 | guòyè | to spend the night |
| 13 | 不能没有 | bùnéngméiyǒu | can't ignore |
| 14 | 吃的文化 | chīdewénhuà | food culture |

# Chapter 13   Weekend Excursions

In ancient times, China's customs were very different from the west. In those days, most of the Chinese were farmers. In a farmer's life it is impossible to follow the seven-day week pattern. When farmers are busy, they are very busy, and only after all the work is done, may they rest. The seven-day week was introduced to China by the west. The six-day work week and one-day rest pattern was learned from the west and only followed by people working in the city and by government employees.

Up until 1994, the city dwellers and the government employees all had a six-day work week and one day off on Sundays. People had very little time for themselves from Monday to Saturday. It was difficult to find time to go shopping or take care of the household. For many people, Sunday was a day to go shopping. As a result, Sunday was the day when the shops were most crowded. Besides shopping, many other things needed to be taken care of as well: the house needed to be cleaned, the clothes washed, and other personal things needed to be dealt with. In fact, people did not really rest on Sundays. Only on the major holidays like the Spring festival, May First, or on National Day could the entire family go out together because they had a two-day holiday. People generally had two days off on major holidays.

Starting in 1994, the five-day work week was introduced, which meant there were two days off on the weekend. At first, the people were not used to it. Because they suddenly had an extra day off, they didn't know what to do. However, very quickly the people started enjoying this pattern for work and life. Nowadays, the residents of Beijing have lots of activities on the weekends. People either handle their personal matters or they go out to have fun with their friends. They cook delicious meals and then enjoy eating them. If they don't feel like doing anything at all, they can simply stay at home and relax.

Because there is more time on the weekends, many families go out on excursions together. They use this time for the whole family to talk and rest and be with one another. A lot of families enjoy going to Xiang Shan (Fragrant Mountain). Xiang Shan is a mountain on the outskirts of Beijing. It is a tall and big and exceptionally beautiful mountain. From the top of the mountain one can see great distances. One can also see the city of Beijing and other sights, such as the Summer Palace and Kunming Lake. In fall, the red leaves on Xiang Shan are the prettiest. Many people come in fall to see Xiang Shan's famous red leaves. Even the emperor used to sightsee on Xiang Shan in former times.

Some families enjoy themselves at Tian Tan (Temple of Heaven). Tian Tan means "large platform." The ancient emperors used this temple to worship heaven and earth. Different temples were used for different ceremonies. The emperors had many temples in Beijing.

Tian Tan is in the south of Beijing, Di Tan (Temple of the Earth) is in the north of Beijing. There is also a Ri Tan (Temple of the Sun) and Yue Tan (Temple of the Moon). Tian Tan was used for worshipping the heaven and Di Tan was used for worshipping the earth. At the beginning of every year the emperor held a worshipping ceremony for several days. While worshipping heaven, the emperor prayed that God would send blessings to his country in the new year and give his subjects happiness in life.

In ancient times, the emperor believed that the natural world was very powerful and could have great influence over a country. The emperor also believed that there was a God in Heaven and that he was the son of this God. For that reason, only the emperor could hold the heaven worshipping ceremony for his country. The place where the emperor worshipped heaven was inside of a tall pagoda. Because the purpose was to worship heaven, he had to be closer to heaven. When the emperor worshipped at Di Tan, he prayed for a good harvest. The emperor also worshipped the sun and the moon and prayed for good weather and no earthquakes in the new year.

In the east of Beijing there is a place called "Dong Bian Men." Inside Dong Bian Men is a place where the weather and earthquakes could be predicted. In ancient times, there was a scientist who invented an apparatus which could observe changes in the weather and also predict earthquakes. Parents often bring their children there to let them know about and learn from China's ancient scientific history.

In recent years, the way in which people spend their weekends has taken a new turn. Formerly, people spent their weekends going shopping or looking at the new products in the stores. That is why, on the weekends, the streets were filled with people. Sometimes there were so many people that the buses could not pass, and in some places people could not even walk. Nowadays, however, many people don't spend their weekends visiting Beijing's famous sights, instead they go sightseeing outside of the city, they go on excursions.

The famous sights in Beijing are now filled with people from outside of Beijing, or with foreigners, people who have never seen Beijing. They have never seen anything like the Forbidden Palace, the Great Wall, or Tian An Men. The people of Beijing have all seen these places. Now the people of Beijing prefer going to the outskirts where other people don't often go. They like going to places where there are only a few people, or no people at all. Those are quiet places, pretty places -- that kind of beauty is different from the beauty in Beijing. The beauty of Beijing is the beauty of a capital, the beauty outside the city is natural beauty. At times, people even spend the night in the outskirts of the city!

Of course, good food cannot be ignored on the weekends. The Chinese have always been quite formal about food. That is one of the reasons people call Chinese culture a "food culture." For example, when the Chinese get together with their friends, meals are always the most important part of the visit. If they don't eat a meal together, the visit might seem a lot less fun. That is why people used to spend their weekends cooking delicious dishes, then they invited their friends to have a drink, chat, and spend a happy weekend together. It is no longer the same now. People's lives have gotten better day by day. People no longer need to spend a lot of time at home cooking meals. Life has become very convenient and many people just go to a restaurant with their friends. It is also easier to invite people this way. The weekends in Beijing have become much more fun.

# 第十四章　菜市場和個體戶

北京的菜市場是一個人們買賣蔬菜的地方,在八十年代以前,所有的菜市商店都是國家的。私人雖然也可以賣

蔬菜,可是國家商店還是人們主要買菜的地方。那時買新鮮[2]的蔬菜和魚肉並不是一件非常容易的事情。八十年以代後,政府開始讓私人或私人公司在市場上賣東西,從那時開始,就有人到北京的郊外去,向農民買新鮮的蔬菜,買來以後,他們再拿到市場去賣,因為這些蔬菜很新鮮,而且不太貴,所以特別受歡迎。

這樣,私人菜市場的生意就越來越好,買賣的人也越來越多,政府就建起了很大的房子,讓人們在裏面買賣蔬菜。在這裏賣蔬菜的人都是私人的生意或私人公司,他們和國營商店[3]裏的公務人員完全不一樣,人們就叫他們個體戶[4]。

後來,許多行業都有了個體戶,不但有賣蔬菜的個體戶,也有賣衣服的個體戶,有的個體戶賣報紙和雜誌,有的賣飲料水果,在北京有不少個體戶開的飯館,來這些飯館吃飯客人主要是一般老百姓,他們喜歡這裏東西便宜,飯菜的味道也非常可口[5]。

向個體戶買東西,最有意思的就是跟賣東西的主人討價[6]還價[7]。買東西的人,常常是先看看東西好不好,決定要買了,客人就會向主人問價錢,很多時候,客人會告訴主人說,這個東西價錢太貴,個體戶的主人會說他的東西是怎樣的好,價錢是如何地公道,這時,客人就會讓主人過來看，故意[8]對這個東西挑毛病[9]，說有什麼地方不滿意，希望能便宜一點，最後，個體戶就請客人說一個價錢，如果個體戶覺得客人希望的價錢還可以接受，買賣就這樣成交[10]了。

如果主人覺得客人要的價錢太低了，不合理[11]，他就會說出一個價錢，比客人要的高一點，這時，客人會告訴主人，在其他的個體戶那裏，同樣的東西比這裏要便宜，如果主人還是不給便宜的價錢，客人就會去別的地方買，常常個體戶在這個時候就會同意給客戶希望[12]的價錢，讓客人把東西買去。

許多個體戶因為生意做得非常好，幾年裏就賺[13]了許多錢，所以就成立[14]了自己的公司，生意更好的時候，就要請人來幫助自己，後來，個體戶和私人公司越來越多，生意也不再是賣蔬菜水果了。現在，北京很多的個體戶和私人公司都是服務行業，比如：私人學校，私人出租車和私人商店。

最特別的私人公司有一家是南方公司，南方公司的老闆原來是一個一般的個體戶。後來，他有一個機會，買了俄羅斯[15]飛機公司的幾架民用[16]飛機，然後他再把飛機賣給中國的一家航空公司[17]。從那以後，南方公司就變得非常有名，公司的生意也越來越好。

因為中國這幾年的變化，很多的人開始找第二個工作。許多的老師白天在學校裏教書，晚上回家以後，就在夜校幫助有需要的人，學習外語或電腦，也有的人給私人公司或個體戶做各種諮詢[18]服務，北京人叫這種第二個的工作為第二職業[19]。

人們在第二職業裏得到的收入[20]，往往會比他們為國家工作的收入要高很多。但是，人們還是喜歡繼續給國家工作，因為國家能給許多的社會福利[21]。比如：人們在生病的時候，國家會給公務人員看病和吃藥的錢，另外，國家還會給工作人員有房子住。不管怎麼樣，個體戶和第二職業使現代北京人的生活有了很大的變化。

## 閱讀理解

一、什麼是個體戶？
二、在中國個體戶是怎樣來的？
三、政府的商店和私人市場有什麼不同？
四、為什麼說討價和還價錢是很有意思的事情？
五、為什麼很多人在找第二職業？
六、第二職業的收入如何？

# 生字

| | | | | |
|---|---|---|---|---|
| 1 | 蔬菜 | shūcài | ㄕㄨ ㄘㄞˋ | vegetables |
| 2 | 新鮮 | xīnxiān | ㄒㄧㄣ ㄒㄧㄢ | fresh |
| 3 | 國營商店 | guóyíngshāngdiàn | ㄍㄨㄛˊ ㄧㄥˊ ㄕㄤ ㄉㄧㄢˋ | state owned stores |
| 4 | 個體戶 | gètǐhù | ㄍㄜˋ ㄊㄧˇ ㄏㄨˋ | family business |
| 5 | 可口 | kěkǒu | ㄎㄜˇ ㄎㄡˇ | tasty; delicious |
| 6 | 討價 | tǎojià | ㄊㄠˇ ㄐㄧㄚˋ | to ask a price |
| 7 | 還價 | huánjià | ㄏㄨㄢˊ ㄐㄧㄚˋ | to counter-offer |
| 8 | 故意 | gùyì | ㄍㄨˋ ㄧˋ | deliberate |
| 9 | 挑毛病 | tiāomáobìng | ㄊㄧㄠ ㄇㄠˊ ㄅㄧㄥˋ | to point out a deficiency |
| 10 | 成交 | chéngjiāo | ㄔㄥˊ ㄐㄧㄠ | to conclude the transaction |
| 11 | 合理 | hélǐ | ㄏㄜˊ ㄌㄧˇ | reasonable |
| 12 | 希望 | xīwàng | ㄒㄧ ㄨㄤˋ | to hope |
| 13 | 賺 | zhuàn | ㄓㄨㄢˋ | to make a profit; gain |
| 14 | 成立 | chénglì | ㄔㄥˊ ㄌㄧˋ | to set up; to establish |
| 15 | 俄羅斯 | èluósī | ㄜˋ ㄌㄨㄛˊ ㄙ | Russia |
| 16 | 民用 | mínyòng | ㄇㄧㄣˊ ㄩㄥˋ | for civil use |
| 17 | 航空公司 | hángkōnggōngsī | ㄏㄤˊ ㄎㄨㄥ ㄍㄨㄥ ㄙ | airline company |
| 18 | 諮詢 | zīxún | ㄗ ㄒㄩㄣˊ | consulting |
| 19 | 職業 | zhíyè | ㄓˊ ㄧㄝˋ | profession |
| 20 | 收入 | shōurù | ㄕㄡ ㄖㄨˋ | income; earnings |
| 21 | 社會福利 | shèhuìfúlì | ㄕㄜˋ ㄏㄨㄟˋ ㄈㄨˊ ㄌㄧˋ | social benefits |

# 第十四章　菜市场和个体户

北京的菜市场是一个人们买卖蔬菜[1]的地方，在八十年代以前，所有的菜市商店都是国家的。私人虽然也可以卖蔬菜，可是国家商店还是人们主要买菜的地方。那时买新鲜[2]的蔬菜和鱼肉并不是一件非常容易的事情。八十年代后，政府开始让私人或私人公司在市场上卖东西，从那时开始，就有人到北京的郊外去，向农民买新鲜的蔬菜，买来以后，他们再拿到市场去卖，因为这些蔬菜很新鲜，而且不太贵，所以特别受欢迎。

这样，私人菜市场的生意就越来越好，买卖的人也越来越多，政府就建起了很大的房子，让人们在里面买卖蔬菜。在这里卖蔬菜的人都是私人的生意或私人公司，他们和国营商店[3]里的公务人员完全不一样，人们就叫他们个体户[4]。

后来，许多行业都有了个体户，不但有卖蔬菜的个体户，也有卖衣服的个体户，有的个体户卖报纸和杂志，有的卖饮料水果，在北京有不少个体户开的饭馆，来这些饭馆吃饭客人主要是一般老百姓，他们喜欢这里东西便宜，饭菜的味道也非常可口[5]。

向个体户买东西，最有意思的就是跟卖东西的主人讨价[6]还价[7]。买东西的人，常常是先看看东西好不好，决定要买了，客人就会向主人问价钱，很多时候，客人会告诉主人说，这个东西价钱太贵，个体户的主人会说他的东西是怎样的好，价钱是如何地公道，这时，客人就会让主人过来看，故意[8]对这个东西挑毛病[9]，说有什么地方不满意，希望能便宜一点，最后，个体户就请客人说一个价钱，如果个体户觉得客人希望的价钱还可以接受，买卖就这样成交[10]了。

如果主人觉得客人要的价钱太低了，不合理[11]，他就会说出一个价钱，比客人要的高一点，这时，客人会告诉主人，在其他的个体户那里，同样的东西比这里要便宜，如果主人还是不给便宜的价钱，客人就会去别的地方买，常常个体户在这个时候就会同意给客户希望[12]的价钱，让客人把东西买去。

许多个体户因为生意做得非常好，几年里就赚[13]了许多钱，所以就成立[14]了自己的公司，生意更好的时候，就要请人来帮助自己，后来，个体户和私人公司越来越多，生意也不再是卖蔬菜水果了。现在，北京很多的个体户和私人公司都是服务行业，比如：私人学校，私人出租车和私人商店。

最特别的私人公司有一家是南方公司，南方公司的老板原来是一个一般的个体户。后来，他有一个机会，买了俄罗斯[15]飞机公司的几架民用[16]飞机，然后他再把飞机卖给中国的一家航空公司[17]。从那以后，南方公司就变得非常有名，公司的生意也越来越好。

因为中国这几年的变化，很多的人开始找第二个工作。许多的老师白天在学校里教书，晚上回家以后，就在夜校帮助有需要的人，学习外语或电脑，也有的人给私人公司或个体户做各种咨询[18]服务，北京人叫这种第二个的工作为第二职业[19]。

人们在第二职业里得到的收入[20]，往往会比他们为国家工作的收入要高很多。但是，人们还是喜欢继续给国家工作，因为国家能给许多的社会福利[21]。比如：人们在生病的时候，国家会给公务人员看病和吃药的钱，另外，国家还会给工作人员有房子住。不管怎么样，个体户和第二职业使现代北京人的生活有了很大的变化。

## 阅读理解

1. 什么是个体户？
2. 在中国个体户是怎样来的？
3. 政府的商店和私人市场有什么不同？
4. 为什么说讨价和还价钱是很有意思的事情？
5. 为什么很多人在找第二职业？
6. 第二职业的收入如何？

# 生字

| | | | |
|---|---|---|---|
| 1 | 蔬菜 | shūcài | vegetables |
| 2 | 新鲜 | xīnxiān | fresh |
| 3 | 国营商店 | guóyíngshāngdiàn | state owned stores |
| 4 | 个体户 | gètǐhù | family business |
| 5 | 可口 | kěkǒu | tasty; delicious |
| 6 | 讨价 | tǎojià | to ask a price |
| 7 | 还价 | huánjià | to counter-offer |
| 8 | 故意 | gùyì | deliberate |
| 9 | 挑毛病 | tiāomáobìng | to point out a deficiency |
| 10 | 成交 | chéngjiāo | to conclude the transaction |
| 11 | 合理 | hélǐ | reasonable |
| 12 | 希望 | xīwàng | to hope |
| 13 | 赚 | zhuàn | to make a profit; gain |
| 14 | 成立 | chénglì | to set up; to establish |
| 15 | 俄罗斯 | sūlián | Russia |
| 16 | 民用 | mínyòng | for civil use |
| 17 | 航空公司 | hángkōnggōngsī | airline company |
| 18 | 咨询 | zīxún | consulting |
| 19 | 职业 | zhíyè | profession |
| 20 | 收入 | shōurù | income; earnings |
| 21 | 社会福利 | shèhuìfúlì | social benefits |

# Chapter 14   Open Produce Markets and Family Businesses

    The produce markets in Beijing are where people go to buy their vegetables. Up until the 1980s, all the produce stores were state stores. Although individuals could also sell their vegetables, most people went to the state-owned stores to do their shopping. In those days, it was not at all easy to buy fresh vegetables, or fish, or meat. After 1980, the government permitted individuals or privately-owned companies to sell their goods in the market. From then on, some people started going to the Beijing suburbs to buy fresh vegetables directly from the farmers. They then took the vegetables back to their local markets and resold them. Because the vegetables were very fresh and not very expensive, they were especially popular.

    Business improved for the open produce markets and more and more people frequented them. Then the government had a very large building built where people could sell their produce. The sellers were all either independent businesses or privately-owned companies. The people who worked in these open markets were very different from those who worked in the state stores. Open markets were family businesses.

Soon family businesses had all kinds of occupations. Not only did the family businesses sell vegetables, but there were also family businesses selling clothes. Other small businesses sold newspapers and magazines, some sold beverages and fruit. In Beijing, there are many family businesses that have opened restaurants. The majority of the customers who eat in those restaurants are common people. They like the fact that these establishments are inexpensive and that the food is delicious.

When buying something from a family business, it is a lot of fun to bargain. First the buyer looks at the product to see whether it is any good. When he has decided to buy it, he asks the owner about the price. Very often, the customer will say, "That it is too expensive," whereupon the owner of the business may explain how good his product is and how fair the price is. At this point, the customer deliberately points out the product's deficiency and explains why it is not satisfactory in the hope of getting a lower price. Then the owner tells the customer to make an offer. If he accepts the offer, the transaction is concluded.

If the owner doesn't agree with the suggested price and finds it unreasonable, he will propose another price, a little higher than the customer's. The customer might answer that other businesses down the street are selling the same product cheaper. If the owner still doesn't want to lower his price, the customer will go somewhere else to buy his product. Very often, the owners will finally agree to the offer in order to get the customer to buy the product.

Because many of these family businesses have been so successful and have made large profits in just a few years, they have started their own companies. If business gets even better, they hire someone as an assistant to help them. Consequently, the number of family-owned businesses and privately-owned companies increased. These businesses are not limited to selling vegetables and fruit. Now many of the family businesses are service industries: there are private schools, privately-owned taxis, and privately-owned shops.

The most extraordinary private company is the Nanfang Company. Originally, the president had an ordinary family business. The family had an opportunity to buy a passenger airplane from a Russian airplane manufacturing company. Later on, they sold the airplane to a Chinese airline company. The Nanfang company became very famous after this and business improved greatly.

Because China has changed so much in recent years, many people have gone out to look for a second job. Many teachers spend the day teaching in school and in the evening they go to a night school to help people study foreign languages or computer science. Other people work as consultants for family businesses or privately-owned businesses. The people of Beijing call this the second profession.

People can earn a lot of money in these secondary jobs, much more than what they make in their state-appointed jobs. But the people still want to continue working for the state because they receive a lot of benefits. If a government employee gets sick, for example, the state will pay for his or her medical care and medication.

Also, the state provides housing for its employees. In any case, family run businesses and secondary jobs have changed the life in Beijing for good.

---

# 第十五章　北京人和北京話

　　北京人就是在北京出生、長大,並且在北京住過一些時候的人,這樣的人也叫老北京。在北京生活的外地人、外國人和學生一般我們都不叫他們北京人。在北京每天來北京的老年人和中年人不一樣，北京的老年人很有文化傳統。他們知道北京的許多故事，每一條街，每一個胡同都很清楚，所以，和北京的老年人談話，就好像是在聽故事一樣。而北京的中年人不一樣，他們是在北京這個城市裏最重要的人，他們都是在各個公司、工廠、學校、和商業中心裏做重要工作的人，也有很多的中年人是在政府裏工作的人，所以，他們的思想和行為[2]都影響著北京人的社會生活。你和他們談話，就會知道在北京天天發生的大事，你也會知道大多數的北京人在想什麼。

北京的年輕人也是很特別的,他們知道的新東西最快,他們對國外的新鮮事情知道的也很多。他們還有一個很特別的地方，就是他們是影響北京語言變化的主要的一代人[3]，北京語言變化最快的主要是在流行語[4]這個方面。

北京人有一個特別的地方，就是非常隨便。北京人說話很直，容易明白，他們喜歡談天說地[5]，對人也很客氣，和北京人在一起，你不會覺得不舒服。因為普通話是全中國人民都天天用的語言，普通話和北京話差不多，所以，你到了北京不會覺得很不習慣。因為北京每天來來去去的人非常多,你不會覺得自己很特別,是一個外地人或外國人。

但是,北京人常常覺得他們是很特別的。最近一千年來,北京一直是中國的首都,是中國文化的中心,歷史上許多重要的大事都是在這裏發生的。中國政府裏發生的許多事情,北京人都是最先知道的。許多外地人來到北京,經常找北京人談天,想知道最近發生的大事和這些事情對中國社會的影響。

北京人還有一個特別的地方,因爲皇帝也住在北京,所以北京人跟皇帝是分不開的。北京有皇帝住過的房子,就是故宮;有皇帝夏天去休息的地方,就是頤和園;北京附近還有皇帝用來保護國家的牆,就是長城;即使皇帝死了以後,每天還是有成千上萬的人去看他的墓[6]。

因爲這些事情,北京人常常會覺得自己跟外地人不一樣。有時,他們也會因爲自己是北京人而引以爲榮[7],因爲他們的文化生活是別的地方的人不能得到的。有很多北京人到外地去工作,不管在外面多少年,還是很喜歡告訴別人自己是北京人,他們也希望有一天能回北京。外地人在北京住久了,也喜歡把自己說成是北京人,他們的語言也真的變得像北京人了。

北京話和普通話很像，北京話只有北京人才會說，普通話是全中國的人都用的語言。北京人能夠聽懂普通話，可是會說普通話的人不一定能聽懂北京話。有時你會覺得，北京人不會說普通話，因為北京人說的話外地人很難聽懂，有很重的北京地方口音[8]。比如：北京人說話的時候喜歡用"兒"字。普通話說"在東邊"，而北京話卻說"在東邊兒"；普通話說"去玩"，而北京話卻說"去玩兒"；普通話說"一點東西"，而北京話卻說"一點兒東西"。

老的北京話是非常好聽的，現在人們已經不常常聽到了，因為北京的變化很大，住在北京的人也和以前不一樣了。老的北京話有一個特別的地方，就是非常的客氣。如果一個老北京請你幫助，他會說"勞駕[9]"；如果老北京請你讓路[10]給他，他就會說"借光[11]"；如果老北京問你的年紀，他就會說"您多大歲數"，而不會說"你幾歲"。

但是，現在的北京話不僅變化很大，而且[12]變化很快，變化最大最快的是北京的流行[13]語。流行語就是在北京街道上和胡同裏人們常常聽到的話，這些話就像流水一樣，每天流來流去，人們聽的多，說的少，因為它不是北京人天天說的話，它是一種口頭語[14]，是北京的年輕人用的最多的。這些年輕人發現社會上的一件新的事情，就用新的口頭語把它表現出來。比如：北京的流行語把外國人叫做"老外[15]"，後來又把什麼都不懂的人也叫做"老外"。這些流行語每天都出現很多，有的不好，人們就不常用它，後來就不再聽到了。有的很好，很多人用它，所以就成了北京人常用的口頭語。

## 閱讀理解

一、什麼樣的人是北京人？
二、北京每天來往的人口有多少？
三、北京話有什麼特別的地方？
四、北京話就是普通話嗎？為什麼？
五、什麼是流行語？
六、什麼叫口頭語？

# 生字

| | | | | |
|---|---|---|---|---|
| 1 | 流動 | liúdòng | ㄌㄧㄡˊ ㄉㄨㄥˋ | to flow; to be on the move |
| 2 | 行爲 | xíngwéi | ㄒㄧㄥˊ ㄨㄟˊ | behavior |
| 3 | 一代人 | yīdàirén | ㄧ ㄉㄞˋ ㄖㄣˊ | one generation |
| 4 | 流行語 | liúxíngyǔ | ㄌㄧㄡˊ ㄒㄧㄥˊ ㄩˇ | slang |
| 5 | 談天說地 | tántiānshuōdì | ㄊㄢˊ ㄊㄧㄢ ㄕㄨㄛ ㄉㄧˋ | to talk about everything under the sun; chat |
| 6 | 墓 | mù | ㄇㄨˋ | grave; tomb |
| 7 | 引以爲榮 | yǐnyǐwéiróng | ㄧㄣˇ ㄧˇ ㄨㄟˊ ㄖㄨㄥˊ | to be proud of |
| 8 | 口音 | kǒuyīn | ㄎㄡˇ ㄧㄣ | accent |
| 9 | 勞駕 | láojià | ㄌㄠˊ ㄐㄧㄚˋ | may I trouble you |
| 10 | 讓路 | rànglù | ㄖㄤˋ ㄌㄨˋ | to make way for somebody |
| 11 | 借光 | jièguāng | ㄐㄧㄝˋ ㄍㄨㄤ | would you mind stepping to one side, please? |
| 12 | 不僅…而且… | bùjǐn…érqiě… | ㄅㄨˋ ㄐㄧㄣˇ… ㄦˊ ㄑㄧㄝˇ… | not only … but also… |
| 13 | 流行 | liúxíng | ㄌㄧㄡˊ ㄒㄧㄥˊ | popular |
| 14 | 口頭語 | kǒutóuyǔ | ㄎㄡˇ ㄊㄡˊ ㄩˇ | oral language |
| 15 | 老外 | lǎowài | ㄌㄠˇ ㄨㄞˋ | slang word for foreigner; layperson |

# 第十五章　北京人和北京话

　　北京人就是在北京出生、长大，并且在北京住过一些时候的人，这样的人也叫老北京。在北京生活的外地人、外国人和学生一般我们都不叫他们北京人。在北京每天来来去去的流动[1]人口有几百万，北京是世界上最大的城市之一。

　　北京的老年人和中年人不一样，北京的老年人很有文化传统。他们知道北京的许多故事，每一条街，每一个胡同都很清楚，所以，和北京的老年人谈话，就好像是在听故事一样。而北京的中年人不一样，他们是在北京这个城市里最重要的人，他们都是在各个公司、工厂、学校、和商业中心里做重要工作的人，也有很多的中年人是在政府里工作的人，所以，他们的思想和行为[2]都影响着北京人的社会生活。你和他们谈话，就会知道在北京天天发生的大事，你也会知道大多数的北京人在想什么。

北京的年轻人也是很特别的,他们知道的新东西最快,他们对国外的新鲜事情知道的也很多。他们还有一个很特别的地方,就是他们是影响北京语言变化的主要的一代人[3],北京语言变化最快的主要是在流行语[4]这个方面。

北京人有一个特别的地方,就是非常随便。北京人说话很直,容易明白,他们喜欢谈天说地[5],对人也很客气,和北京人在一起,你不会觉得不舒服。因为普通话是全中国人民都天天用的语言,普通话和北京话差不多,所以,你到了北京不会觉得很不习惯。因为北京每天来来去去的人非常多,你不会觉得自己很特别,是一个外地人或外国人。

但是,北京人常常觉得他们是很特别的。最近一千年来,北京一直是中国的首都,是中国文化的中心,历史上许多重要的大事都是在这里发生的。中国政府里发生的许多事情,北京人都是最先知道的。许多外地人来到北京,经常找北京人谈天,想知道最近发生的大事和这些事情对中国社会的影响。

北京人还有一个特别的地方,因为皇帝也住在北京,所以北京人跟皇帝是分不开的。北京有皇帝住过的房子,就是故宫;有皇帝夏天去休息的地方,就是颐和园;北京附近还有皇帝用来保护国家的墙，就是长城；即使皇帝死了以后，每天还是有成千上万的人去看他的墓[6]。

因为这些事情，北京人常常会觉得自己跟外地人不一样。有时，他们也会因为自己是北京人而引以为荣[7]，因为他们的文化生活是别的地方的人不能得到的。有很多北京人到外地去工作，不管在外面多少年，还是很喜欢告诉别人自己是北京人，他们也希望有一天能回北京。外地人在北京住久了，也喜欢把自己说成是北京人，他们的语言也真的变得像北京人了。

北京话和普通话很像，北京话只有北京人才会说，普通话是全中国的人都用的语言。北京人能够听懂普通话，可是会说普通话的人不一定能听懂北京话。有时你会觉得，北京人不会说普通话，因为北京人说的话外地人很难听懂，有很重的北京地方口音[8]。比如：北京人说话的时候喜欢用"儿"字。普通话说"在东边"，而北京话却说"在东边儿"；普通话说"去玩"，而北京话却说"去玩儿"；普通话说"一点东西"，而北京话却说"一点儿东西"。

老的北京话是非常好听的，现在人们已经不常常听到了，因为北京的变化很大，住在北京的人也和以前不一样了。老的北京话有一个特别的地方，就是非常的客气。如果一个老北京请你帮助,他会说"劳驾[9]";如果老北京请你让路[10]给他,他就会说"借光[11]";如果老北京问你的年纪,他就会说"您多大岁数",而不会说"你几岁"。

但是,现在的北京话不仅变化很大,而且[12]变化很快,变化最大最快的是北京的流行[13]语。流行语就是在北京街道上和胡同里人们常常听到的话,这些话就像流水一样,每天流来流去,人们听的多,说的少,因为它不是北京人天天说的话,它是一种口头语[14],是北京的年轻人用的最多的。这些年轻人发现社会上的一件新的事情,就用新的口头语把它表现出来。比如:北京的流行语把外国人叫做"老外[15]",后来又把什么都不懂的人也叫做"老外"。这些流行语每天都出现很多,有的不好,人们就不常用它,后来就不再听到了。有的很好,很多人用它,所以就成了北京人常用的口头语。

# 阅读理解

1. 什么样的人是北京人？
2. 北京每天来往的人口有多少？
3. 北京话有什么特别的地方？
4. 北京话就是普通话吗？为什么？
5. 什么是流行语？
6. 什么叫口头语？

# 生字

| | | | |
|---|---|---|---|
| 1 | 流动 | liúdòng | to flow; to be on the move |
| 2 | 行为 | xíngwéi | behavior |
| 3 | 一代人 | yīdàirén | one generation |
| 4 | 流行语 | liúxíngyǔ | slang |
| 5 | 谈天说地 | tántiānshuōdì | to talk about everything under the sun; chat |
| 6 | 墓 | mù | grave; tomb |
| 7 | 引以为荣 | yǐnyǐwéiróng | to be proud of |
| 8 | 口音 | kǒuyīn | accent |
| 9 | 劳驾 | láojià | may I trouble you |
| 10 | 让路 | rànglù | to make way for somebody |
| 11 | 借光 | jièguāng | would you mind stepping to one side, please? |
| 12 | 不仅…而且… | bùjǐn…érqiě… | not only … but also… |
| 13 | 流行 | liúxíng | popular |
| 14 | 口头语 | kǒutóuyǔ | oral language |
| 15 | 老外 | lǎowài | slang word for foreigner; layperson |

# Chapter 15  The People of Beijing and the Beijing Dialect

"Beijing People" are those who were born, grew up, and have spent most of their time in Beijing. They are also called "Old Beijing Residents." People living in Beijing who are from other parts of China -- or foreigners and students -- generally aren't called Beijing People. The people who come in and out of Beijing everyday number over several million. Beijing is one of the biggest cities in the world

The elderly residents of Beijing are different from the middle-aged ones. The elderly still know the traditional culture. They know many stories about Beijing, they know every street and Hu Tong intimately. Talking to the elderly is like listening to a storyteller. Beijing's middle-aged residents are not like the elderly. The middle-aged residents are the most important group in the city. They all have important jobs in either a company, a factory, a school, or a trade center. Many of the middle-aged people also work for the government. Their actions and behavior have a great influence on the life of the community. Talking to them you can find out what goes on in Beijing everyday. You can also find out what the majority of Beijing people are thinking.

The young people of Beijing are quite special too. They find out about the newest things very fast. They know all about foreign novelties. Another special aspect of the youth is that they are the generation that has the greatest influence on the linguistic changes in Beijing. Beijing's slang changes very fast.

Another characteristic of the Beijing people is the fact that they are very informal. Their speech is very straightforward and easy to understand. They like to talk about everything under the sun, and are very polite to people. When you get together with people from Beijing, you'll never feel uncomfortable. Standard Chinese is the language spoken by Chinese people everywhere in the country. Standard Chinese and Beijing Dialect are very similar and you will not feel frustrated by it. Because there are so many people coming and going in and out of Beijing, you won't feel that you don't fit in because you are from another part of China or from another country.

However, the Beijing people do feel that they are unusual. For the last thousand years, Beijing has been the capital and is the center of China's culture. Many important historical events happened there. When something happens in the government, the people of Beijing are the first to know. When people from other parts of China come to Beijing, they often seek out some local residents who will tell them what they want to know about important current events and about their influence on Chinese society.

Another particularity is that because the emperor lived in Beijing, the people of Beijing and the ancient emperors cannot be separated.

The Forbidden City, which was the emperor's home, is located in Beijing; the Summer Palace, the emperor's summer resort, is also in Beijing. The Great Wall of China, which protected the country, is also near Beijing. Even after the emperor's death, millions of people went to visit his grave everyday.

For all these reasons, the people of Beijing believe that they are different from others. Sometimes they even feel proud to be from Beijing because people from other places can't attain the same level of culture. Some people of Beijing go to work in other parts of China, but no matter how long they stay away, they always enjoy telling people that they are from Beijing and that they wish to return home some day. Chinese from other parts of China who have lived in Beijing for awhile also like to call themselves Beijing people. Even their dialects change so that they begin to sound like Beijing people.

The Beijing dialect is very similar to standard Chinese. The Beijing dialect is only spoken in Beijing, whereas standard Chinese is spoken all over the country. The people from Beijing can understand standard Chinese, but those who speak standard Chinese don't necessarily understand the Beijing dialect. Sometimes it seems as if the Beijing residents can't speak standard Chinese because their language can be hard to understand by outsiders when spoken with a strong local accent. In Beijing, the people like to add an "r" sound to their speech. For example, in standard Chinese, we would say "zai dong bian," but in Beijing dialect, we would say "zai dong bianr." In standard Chinese, we say "qu wan," which would be "qu wanr" in Beijing. In standard Chinese, we say "yi dian dongxi," in Beijing dialect, it is "yi dianr dongxi."

The old Beijing dialect is pleasant to listen to, but it isn't often heard anymore because Beijing has changed so much. The residents of Beijing are not the same as before. The language of Beijing used to be particularly courteous. For example, if an Old Beijing Resident asked you for help, he would say "lao jia" (May I trouble you?). Or if an Old Beijing Resident wanted you to move out of his way, he may say "jie guang" (Would you mind stepping to one side please?). If an Old Beijing Resident asked you your age, he would say, "nin duo da sui shu" (Would you mind telling me your age?) and not "ni ji sui" (How old are you?).

The Beijing dialect has changed a lot and the change happened quickly. The major changes and the most rapid ones occurred in Beijing's slang. Slang is the language often heard on the streets and in the Hu Tong. Slang flows in and out of the language just like water. The people hear it often but only rarely use it, because it is not the most common language. It is an oral language used mainly by the youth of Beijing. When they discover a novelty of some kind, they use their oral language to describe it. For example, in slang, the word for foreigner is "lao wai;" later, the same words were used for anyone who didn't have any knowledge of something. These new slang expressions evolve all the time. If they aren't good, they aren't used for very long, and sooner or later one doesn't hear them anymore.

Some expressions are excellent and they then become part of Beijing's oral language.

# 第十六章　變化中的北京

中國是一個非常古老的國家,有幾千年的歷史。同時中國也是世界上人口最多的國家。雖然在古時候,中國的皇帝和世界上別的國家有一些來往,可是幾千年來,中國可以說是一個把自己關起來的國家。只是從八十年代開始，中國才決定開放自己，向西方國家學習，發展中國的經濟[1]。

從八十年代到今天，北京發生了很大的變化。變化最大的地方是北京最重要的街道——長安街，七十年代以前，長安街上沒有地鐵。現在，人們不管是去天安門廣場、故宮遊覽，還是去王府井，都可以坐地鐵去，有了地鐵，交通就方便多了。

所以，北京的街道和交通的變化是很大的。北京的街道早在七百多年前就建得非常好了，當時北京分大街、小街、和胡同。大街有二十四步寬，小街有十二步寬，胡同就很小了。而現在，北京的街道很多都變寬變新了，新的街道越來越多。，北京的街道還有一個特別的變化，就是新建了很多的環城公路[2]和立交橋[3]。環城公路和立交橋使北京的交通發生了很大的變化，使北京的交通更快更方便，過去，從北京市到國際機場[4]，開車需要一個多小時，而現在，開車去飛機場只需要二十幾分鐘。

交通的變化是因為北京的汽車一年比一年多。在北京的大街上，各個國家的汽車到處都是，像流水一樣。其中以德國[5]、美國和日本的汽車最多，坐出租汽車的人也越來越多。在北京每一條主要的街道上，你隨時[6]都可以看到出租汽車。

很多的北京人都希望有一天能有自己的私人小汽車，中國政府現在正和許多外國汽車公司一起開發[7]中國的汽車市場。最近十幾年內，許多外國汽車公司已經和中國政府一起在生產小汽車。不難想像[8]得到，將來有一天私人小汽車在北京變得越來越多。

北京城市的另一個大的變化，是新建了許多的高樓。這些新建的大樓，有些是辦公大樓[9]，有些是商業中心，還有的是國際飯店。在這些高樓裏，有很多的外國公司在那裏辦公。近二十年來，中國的開放使許許多多的外國公司對中國的市場產生了很大的興趣。許多的外國大公司都到中國來開分公司[10]，因為中國是世界上最大的市場。

在這些外國公司裏，北京人最歡迎的是美國快餐，世界上最大美國快餐店就在中國。在八十年代，外國快餐開始進到中國市場，而且發展非常快，其中有意大利[11]的比薩餅[12]和美國的麥當勞漢堡[13]。美國的快餐店在中國最多，發展也最快，離天安門不遠，就是麥當勞快餐店，每天都有許多的年輕人喜歡到這裏來吃一吃，現在，北京已經有五家麥當勞漢堡分店[14]。

來到中國的美國快餐店中，美國肯德基[15]炸雞[16]是最早的，在中國開的分店也是最多的，也許，中國現代式的快餐是從肯德基開始發展起來的。因為生意非常好，所以，一到周末，人們就在肯德基炸雞店的門前站起了長隊[17]，排隊的人非常的多。其實北京人吃肯德基不完全是因為對外來的東西好奇[18]，而是因為北京人的生活越來越快，吃飯的習慣也有了改變。所以，很多的中國餐館也開始做起快餐來，現在北京的快餐越來越多了。

這些年來，北京人家裏的變化也很大。八十年代以前，北京人的家庭裏有黑白電視[19]的還不是很多，大多數的北京人家裏是沒有電話[20]的。從八十年代開始，人們的生活水平越來越好。現在，很多家庭都有了彩色電視[21]，許多人的家裏也有了私人電話。

現代的新東西在北京越來越多。有的東西剛剛在美國生產[22]出來，你在北京就可以看見，比如手提[23]電話已經有很多人天天在用了。許多外國人到北京來，都感覺到在變化中的北京，希望有一天北京能變得更好。

## 閱讀理解

一、你認爲北京最大的變化在那一個方面？

二、北京的交通有什麼大變化？

三、爲什麼說中國是世界上最大的市場國？

四、爲什麼年輕人喜歡吃西方快餐？

五、中國人的家庭發生了那些變化？

六、北京的將來會變得更好嗎？

七、你對中國的開放有什麼看法？

八、中國在變化中最需要什麼幫助？

九、你覺得你將來有機會去中國嗎？

## 生字

| | | | | |
|---|---|---|---|---|
| 1 | 經濟 | jīngjì | ㄐㄧㄥ ㄐㄧˋ | economy |
| 2 | 環城公路 | huánchéng gōnglù | ㄏㄨㄢˊ ㄔㄥˊ ㄍㄨㄥ ㄌㄨˋ | highway encircling the city |
| 3 | 立交橋 | lìjiāoqiáo | ㄌㄧˋ ㄐㄧㄠ ㄑㄧㄠˊ | overpass |
| 4 | 國際機場 | guójìjīcháng | ㄍㄨㄛˊ ㄐㄧˋ ㄐㄧ ㄔㄤˊ | international airport |
| 5 | 德國 | déguó | ㄉㄜˊ ㄍㄨㄛˊ | Germany |
| 6 | 隨時 | suíshí | ㄙㄨㄟˊ ㄕˊ | any time |
| 7 | 開發 | kāifā | ㄎㄞ ㄈㄚ | to develop |

| | | | | |
|---|---|---|---|---|
| 8 | 想像 | xiǎngxiàng | ㄒㄧㄤˇ ㄒㄧㄤˋ | to imagine |
| 9 | 辦公大樓 | bàngōngdàlóu | ㄅㄢˋ ㄍㄨㄥ ㄉㄚˋ ㄌㄡˊ | office building |
| 10 | 分公司 | fēngōngsī | ㄈㄣ ㄍㄨㄥ ㄙ | branch (of a business) |
| 11 | 意大利 | yìdàlì | ㄧˋ ㄉㄚˋ ㄌㄧˋ | Italy |
| 12 | 比薩餅 | bǐsàbǐng | ㄅㄧˇ ㄙㄚˋ ㄅㄧㄥˇ | Pizza |
| 13 | 漢堡 | hànbǎo | ㄏㄢˋ ㄅㄠˇ | hamburger |
| 14 | 分店 | fēndiàn | ㄈㄣ ㄉㄧㄢˋ | store |
| 15 | 肯德基 | kěndéjī | ㄎㄣˇ ㄉㄜˊ ㄐㄧ | Kentucky |
| 16 | 炸雞 | zhéjī | ㄓㄚˋ ㄐㄧ | fried chicken |
| 17 | 長隊 | chángduì | ㄔㄤˊ ㄉㄨㄟˋ | a long line |
| 18 | 好奇 | hàoqí | ㄏㄠˇ ㄑㄧˊ | to be curious about |
| 19 | 黑白電視 | hēibáidiànshì | ㄏㄟ ㄅㄞˊ ㄉㄧㄢˋ ㄕˋ | black and white TV |
| 20 | 電話 | diànhuà | ㄉㄧㄢˋ ㄏㄨㄚˋ | telephone |
| 21 | 彩色電視 | cǎisèdiànshì | ㄘㄞˇ ㄙㄜˋ ㄉㄧㄢˋ ㄕˋ | color TV |
| 22 | 生產 | shēngchǎn | ㄕㄥ ㄔㄢˇ | to manufacture |
| 23 | 手提 | shǒutí | ㄕㄡˇ ㄊㄧˊ | portable |

# 第十六章　变化中的北京

中国是一个非常古老的国家，有几千年的历史。同时中国也是世界上人口最多的国家。虽然在古时候，中国的皇帝和世界上别的国家有一些来往，可是几千年来，中国可以说是一个把自己关起来的国家。只是从八十年代开始，中国才决定开放自己，向西方国家学习，发展中国的经济[1]。

从八十年代到今天，北京发生了很大的变化。变化最大的地方是北京最重要的街道——长安街，七十年代以前，长安街上没有地铁。现在，人们不管是去天安门广场、故宫游览，还是去王府井，都可以坐地铁去，有了地铁，交通就方便多了。

所以，北京的街道和交通的变化是很大的。北京的街道早在七百多年前就建得非常好了，当时北京分大街、小街、和胡同。大街有二十四步宽，小街有十二步宽，胡同就很小了。而现在，北京的街道很多都变宽变新了，新的街道越来越多。，北京的街道还有一个特别的变化，就是新建了很多的环城公路[2]和立交桥[3]。环城公路和立交桥使北京的交通发生了很大的变化，使北京的交通更快更方便，过去，从北京市到国际机场[4]，开车需要一个多小时，而现在，开车去飞机场只需要二十几分钟。

交通的变化是因为北京的汽车一年比一年多。在北京的大街上，各个国家的汽车到处都是，像流水一样。其中以德国[5]、美国和日本的汽车最多，坐出租汽车的人也越来越多。在北京每一条主要的街道上，你随时[6]都可以看到出租汽车。

很多的北京人都希望有一天能有自己的私人小汽车，中国政府现在正和许多外国汽车公司一起开发[7]中国的汽车市场。最近十几年内，许多外国汽车公司已经和中国政府一起在生产小汽车。不难想像[8]得到，将来有一天私人小汽车在北京变得越来越多。

北京城市的另一个大的变化，是新建了许多的高楼。这些新建的大楼，有些是办公大楼[9]，有些是商业中心，还有的是国际饭店。在这些高楼里，有很多的外国公司在那里办公。近二十年来，中国的开放使许许多多的外国公司对中国的市场产生了很大的兴趣。许多的外国大公司都到中国来开分公司[10]，因为中国是世界上最大的市场。

在这些外国公司里，北京人最欢迎的是美国快餐，世界上最大美国快餐店就在中国。在八十年代，外国快餐开始进到中国市场，而且发展非常快，其中有意大利[11]的比萨饼[12]和美国的麦当劳汉堡[13]。美国的快餐店在中国最多，发展也最快，离天安门不远，就是麦当劳快餐店，每天都有许多的年轻人喜欢到这里来吃一吃，现在，北京已经有五家麦当劳汉堡分店[14]。

来到中国的美国快餐店中，美国肯德基[15]炸鸡[16]是最早的，在中国开的分店也是最多的，也许，中国现代式的快餐是从肯德基开始发展起来的。因为生意非常好，所以，一到周末，人们就在肯德基炸鸡店的门前站起了长队[17]，排队的人非常的多。其实北京人吃肯德基不完全是因为对外来的东西好奇[18]，而是因为北京人的生活越来越快，吃饭的习惯也有了改变。所以，很多的中国餐馆也开始做起快餐来，现在北京的快餐越来越多了。

这些年来，北京人家里的变化也很大。八十年代以前，北京人的家庭里有黑白电视[19]的还不是很多，大多数的北京人家里是没有电话[20]的。从八十年代开始，人们的生活水平越来越好。现在，很多家庭都有了彩色电视[21]，许多人的家里也有了私人电话。

现代的新东西在北京越来越多。有的东西刚刚在美国生产[22]出来，你在北京就可以看见，比如手提[23]电话已经有很多人天天在用了。许多外国人到北京来，都感觉到在变化中的北京，希望有一天北京能变得更好。

## 阅读理解

1. 你认为北京最大的变化在那一个方面？
2. 北京的交通有什么大变化？
3. 为什么说中国是世界上最大的市场国？
4. 为什么年轻人喜欢吃西方快餐？
5. 中国人的家庭发生了那些变化？
6. 北京的将来会变得更好吗？
7. 你对中国的开放有什么看法？
8. 中国在变化中最需要什么帮助？
9. 你觉得你将来有机会去中国吗？

## 生字

| | | | |
|---|---|---|---|
| 1 | 经济 | jīngjì | economy |
| 2 | 环城公路 | huánchénggōnglù | highway encircling the city |
| 3 | 立交桥 | lìjiāoqiáo | overpass |
| 4 | 国际机场 | guójìjīchǎng | international airport |
| 5 | 德国 | déguó | Germany |
| 6 | 随时 | suíshí | any time |
| 7 | 开发 | kāifā | to develop |
| 8 | 想像 | xiǎngxiàng | to imagine |
| 9 | 办公大楼 | bàngōngdàlóu | office building |
| 10 | 分公司 | fēngōngsī | branch (of a business) |
| 11 | 意大利 | yìdàlì | Italy |
| 12 | 比萨饼 | bǐsàbǐng | Pizza |
| 13 | 汉堡 | hànbǎo | hamburger |
| 14 | 分店 | fēndiàn | store |
| 15 | 肯德基 | kěndéjī | Kentucky |
| 16 | 炸鸡 | zhájī | fried chicken |
| 17 | 长队 | chángduì | a long line |
| 18 | 好奇 | hàoqí | to be curious about |
| 19 | 黑白电视 | hēibáidiànshì | black and white TV |
| 20 | 电话 | diànhuà | telephone |
| 21 | 彩色电视 | cǎisèdiànshì | color TV |
| 22 | 生产 | shēngchǎn | to manufacture |
| 23 | 手提 | shǒutí | portable |

# Chapter 16: Changing Beijing

China is a very ancient country, it has a history of several thousand years. It is also the country with the largest population in the world. Although there was some contact between the emperor of China and other countries in ancient times, for several thousand years China has been closed to the outside world. Only in the 1980s did China decide to open up to the West and to learn from the West and to develop its economy.

From 1980 up until today, Beijing has undergone a great change. The biggest change occurred on Beijing's main avenue, Chang An Jie (Avenue of Eternal Peace). Before the 1970s, there was no subway along Chang An Jie. Nowadays, whether people are going to Tian An Men Square, sightseeing in the Forbidden City, or going to Wang Fu Jing, they can take the subway. Having a subway made public transportation much more convenient.

Beijing's streets and transportation have changed enormously. The streets that were built over 700 years ago were well-built. In those days, the streets of Beijing were divided into large and small streets and Hu Tong (alleys). The large streets were twenty-four strides wide, the small streets were twelve strides wide, and the Hu Tong were very thin. Now many of Beijing's streets have been widened and renovated. There are also more and more new streets. There is another important change, many of the newly built roads are highways encircling the city with overpasses. Those highways and overpasses brought on major changes to traffic in Beijing, transportation became faster and more convenient. It used to take over one hour to get to the international airport, now it takes just over twenty minutes to drive to the airport.

The reason for the traffic changes is that there are more cars in Beijing every year. On the main streets of Beijing there are cars from all over: from Germany, from America, and mainly from Japan. More and more people are taking taxis as well. On any major street in Beijing there are taxis at any time.

Many residents of Beijing long to have their own car some day. The Chinese government is currently working with foreign automobile companies to develop China's automobile industry. In the last ten years, many foreign automobile companies have manufactured cars with China. It is not hard to imagine that some day in the future there will be many more privately-owned cars in Beijing.

Another big change in Beijing is the many high-rises that have been built. Some of these newly built high-rises are office buildings, some are shopping centers, and some are international hotels. There are many foreign businesses in those buildings. In the last twenty years, the opening of China has caused many foreign companies to develop an interest in the Chinese market. Many large foreign companies came to China to open a branch of their business because China is the largest market in the world.

The companies that the people like best among all the foreign companies are the American fast-food companies. The largest American fast-food restaurant in the world happens to be in China. In the 1980s, these fast-food restaurants started to break into the Chinese market. They developed very quickly. Among them were Italian pizza and American McDonalds hamburgers. In China, most of the fast-food restaurants are American, they developed the fastest. Not far from Tian An Men is where McDonalds is located. Everyday, many young people go to eat there. There are now five McDonalds restaurants in Beijing.

The first American fast-food restaurant to come to China was Kentucky Fried Chicken. Kentucky Fried Chicken also has the most restaurants in China. China's modern fast-food style probably started with Kentucky Fried Chicken. Business is so good that on the weekends there is a long line in front of the Kentucky Fried Chicken restaurant. There are many, many people who eat there. In Beijing, the people don't eat Kentucky Fried Chicken solely because they are curious about foreign things, but also because the pace of life is faster and eating customs have changed. Consequently, many Chinese restaurants have started serving fast-food as well. There are now more and more fast-food places in Beijing.

In recent years, life within the family has also undergone a change. Before the 1980s, not many families had a black and white television in their home. The majority of the homes did not have telephones. Since the '80s, living standards have improved. Now many families have color television and many also have private telephones in their homes.

More and more new products are being introduced into Beijing. Sometimes these products are available in Beijing as soon as they have been manufactured in America. Cell phones, for example, are already being used by many. When foreigners come to Beijing they will see Beijing in the midst of change. Some hope that things will get even better in the future

# 附錄一 本書使用頻率最高的 500 個字

（後面數字為出現次數）

| | | | | | | | | | |
|---|---|---|---|---|---|---|---|---|---|
| 的 | 1383 | 不 | 202 | 年 | 134 | 樣 | 86 | 後 | 71 |
| 是 | 542 | 以 | 198 | 皇 | 121 | 城 | 85 | 店 | 68 |
| 人 | 536 | 和 | 197 | 會 | 119 | 西 | 84 | 事 | 67 |
| 京 | 423 | 裏 | 185 | 為 | 117 | 活 | 84 | 話 | 66 |
| 有 | 411 | 天 | 182 | 自 | 111 | 最 | 84 | 起 | 65 |
| 北 | 369 | 都 | 180 | 候 | 111 | 老 | 82 | 代 | 64 |
| 在 | 354 | 時 | 178 | 車 | 110 | 長 | 82 | 開 | 62 |
| 多 | 292 | 學 | 170 | 去 | 109 | 每 | 80 | 節 | 62 |
| 很 | 282 | 方 | 168 | 吃 | 107 | 劇 | 80 | 同 | 61 |
| 國 | 281 | 地 | 162 | 可 | 103 | 小 | 79 | 面 | 61 |
| 這 | 259 | 他 | 160 | 帝 | 102 | 還 | 79 | 府 | 60 |
| 們 | 251 | 生 | 153 | 些 | 94 | 化 | 77 | 道 | 60 |
| 了 | 250 | 常 | 152 | 看 | 94 | 好 | 77 | 歡 | 60 |
| 個 | 240 | 也 | 149 | 許 | 92 | 古 | 76 | 出 | 59 |
| 來 | 230 | 上 | 143 | 門 | 88 | 東 | 76 | 變 | 59 |
| 大 | 224 | 到 | 140 | 越 | 88 | 因 | 75 | 做 | 58 |
| 中 | 223 | 要 | 137 | 子 | 86 | 所 | 75 | 從 | 58 |
| 就 | 209 | 家 | 136 | 現 | 86 | 行 | 73 | 外 | 57 |

| 字 | 次 | 字 | 次 | 字 | 次 | 字 | 次 | 字 | 次 | 字 | 次 | 字 | 次 | 字 | 次 |
|---|---|---|---|---|---|---|---|---|---|---|---|---|---|---|---|
| 名 | 57 | 間 | 42 | 書 | 34 | 下 | 28 | 千 | 23 | | | | | | |
| 公 | 56 | 叫 | 41 | 動 | 34 | 走 | 28 | 它 | 23 | | | | | | |
| 市 | 56 | 如 | 41 | 飯 | 34 | 表 | 28 | 全 | 23 | | | | | | |
| 非 | 56 | 作 | 41 | 客 | 33 | 孩 | 28 | 見 | 23 | | | | | | |
| 己 | 55 | 政 | 41 | 校 | 33 | 給 | 28 | 念 | 23 | | | | | | |
| 安 | 55 | 高 | 41 | 演 | 33 | 對 | 28 | 想 | 23 | | | | | | |
| 說 | 55 | 建 | 40 | 比 | 32 | 把 | 27 | 戶 | 22 | | | | | | |
| 日 | 54 | 特 | 40 | 坐 | 32 | 果 | 27 | 世 | 22 | | | | | | |
| 過 | 53 | 麼 | 40 | 知 | 32 | 近 | 27 | 定 | 22 | | | | | | |
| 街 | 52 | 民 | 39 | 重 | 32 | 息 | 27 | 花 | 22 | | | | | | |
| 喜 | 51 | 第 | 39 | 買 | 32 | 騎 | 27 | 便 | 22 | | | | | | |
| 得 | 50 | 幾 | 39 | 園 | 32 | 邊 | 27 | 條 | 22 | | | | | | |
| 你 | 49 | 賣 | 39 | 像 | 32 | 只 | 26 | 著 | 22 | | | | | | |
| 別 | 49 | 史 | 38 | 才 | 31 | 其 | 26 | 鐵 | 22 | | | | | | |
| 始 | 49 | 成 | 38 | 快 | 31 | 當 | 26 | 界 | 21 | | | | | | |
| 那 | 48 | 夜 | 38 | 路 | 31 | 分 | 26 | 茶 | 21 | | | | | | |
| 用 | 47 | 胡 | 38 | 王 | 30 | 合 | 25 | 覺 | 21 | | | | | | |
| 經 | 47 | 然 | 38 | 字 | 30 | 風 | 25 | 但 | 20 | | | | | | |
| 種 | 46 | 歷 | 38 | 或 | 30 | 晚 | 25 | 私 | 20 | | | | | | |
| 文 | 45 | 汽 | 37 | 習 | 30 | 菜 | 25 | 周 | 20 | | | | | | |
| 主 | 45 | 能 | 37 | 業 | 30 | 輕 | 25 | 電 | 20 | | | | | | |
| 前 | 45 | 情 | 37 | 錢 | 30 | 讓 | 25 | 牆 | 20 | | | | | | |
| 而 | 44 | 新 | 37 | 觀 | 30 | 什 | 24 | 山 | 19 | | | | | | |
| 各 | 43 | 宮 | 36 | 已 | 29 | 司 | 24 | 物 | 19 | | | | | | |
| 場 | 43 | 百 | 35 | 沒 | 29 | 通 | 24 | 教 | 19 | | | | | | |
| 意 | 43 | 發 | 35 | 房 | 29 | 談 | 24 | 頤 | 19 | | | | | | |
| 住 | 42 | 工 | 34 | 思 | 29 | 興 | 24 | 雖 | 19 | | | | | | |
| 院 | 42 | 故 | 34 | 遊 | 29 | 覽 | 24 | 聽 | 19 | | | | | | |
| 商 | 42 | 美 | 34 | 廣 | 29 | | | 體 | 19 | | | | | | |

# 附錄一 本書使用頻率最高的500個字

| 字 | 次 | 字 | 次 | 字 | 次 | 字 | 次 | 字 | 次 |
|---|---|---|---|---|---|---|---|---|---|
| 又 | 18 | 般 | 16 | 父 | 13 | 水 | 11 | 運 | 10 |
| 井 | 18 | 處 | 16 | 正 | 13 | 育 | 11 | 歌 | 10 |
| 友 | 18 | 餐 | 16 | 母 | 13 | 兒 | 11 | 關 | 10 |
| 太 | 18 | 舉 | 16 | 白 | 13 | 迎 | 11 | 之 | 9 |
| 件 | 18 | 麗 | 16 | 向 | 13 | 拜 | 11 | 午 | 9 |
| 再 | 18 | 護 | 15 | 考 | 13 | 流 | 11 | 月 | 9 |
| 放 | 18 | 且 | 15 | 更 | 13 | 郊 | 11 | 另 | 9 |
| 朋 | 18 | 完 | 15 | 容 | 13 | 真 | 11 | 平 | 9 |
| 法 | 18 | 直 | 15 | 帶 | 13 | 普 | 11 | 打 | 9 |
| 租 | 18 | 社 | 15 | 景 | 13 | 華 | 11 | 次 | 9 |
| 唱 | 18 | 者 | 15 | 期 | 13 | 陽 | 11 | 並 | 9 |
| 館 | 18 | 庭 | 15 | 湖 | 13 | 慢 | 11 | 亮 | 9 |
| 少 | 17 | 烤 | 15 | 輪 | 13 | 認 | 11 | 音 | 9 |
| 首 | 17 | 術 | 15 | 點 | 13 | 價 | 11 | 夏 | 9 |
| 員 | 17 | 需 | 15 | 藝 | 13 | 築 | 11 | 務 | 9 |
| 座 | 17 | 影 | 15 | 力 | 12 | 辦 | 11 | 統 | 9 |
| 問 | 17 | 數 | 15 | 口 | 12 | 讀 | 11 | 訪 | 9 |
| 章 | 17 | 樓 | 15 | 使 | 12 | 今 | 11 | 萬 | 9 |
| 號 | 17 | 趣 | 15 | 易 | 12 | 元 | 10 | 試 | 9 |
| 語 | 17 | 壇 | 15 | 明 | 12 | 半 | 10 | 遠 | 9 |
| 鴨 | 17 | 心 | 14 | 玩 | 12 | 位 | 10 | 際 | 9 |
| 末 | 16 | 共 | 14 | 卻 | 12 | 找 | 10 | 蔬 | 9 |
| 交 | 16 | 希 | 14 | 氣 | 12 | 附 | 10 | 久 | 9 |
| 式 | 16 | 兩 | 14 | 班 | 12 | 春 | 10 | 必 | 8 |
| 告 | 16 | 受 | 14 | 訴 | 12 | 星 | 10 | 回 | 8 |
| 姓 | 16 | 保 | 14 | 請 | 12 | 差 | 10 | 助 | 8 |
| 服 | 16 | 展 | 14 | 課 | 12 | 視 | 10 | 我 | 8 |
| 南 | 16 | 接 | 14 | 機 | 12 | 群 | 10 | 怎 | 8 |
| 原 | 16 | 望 | 14 | 女 | 11 | 跟 | 10 | 師 | 8 |

| 8 | | 7 | | 6 | | 5 | | 4 | |
|---|---|---|---|---|---|---|---|---|---|
| 秦 | 8 | 紅 | 7 | 旦 | 6 | 皮 | 5 | 加 | 4 |
| 假 | 8 | 香 | 7 | 言 | 6 | 先 | 5 | 包 | 4 |
| 參 | 8 | 站 | 7 | 呢 | 6 | 忙 | 5 | 石 | 4 |
| 部 | 8 | 馬 | 7 | 奇 | 6 | 兵 | 5 | 收 | 4 |
| 喝 | 8 | 婦 | 7 | 爸 | 6 | 具 | 5 | 死 | 4 |
| 提 | 8 | 理 | 7 | 背 | 6 | 宜 | 5 | 肉 | 4 |
| 等 | 8 | 紹 | 7 | 剛 | 6 | 科 | 5 | 努 | 4 |
| 須 | 8 | 勞 | 7 | 除 | 6 | 消 | 5 | 辛 | 4 |
| 傳 | 8 | 單 | 7 | 將 | 6 | 酒 | 5 | 里 | 4 |
| 實 | 8 | 進 | 7 | 族 | 6 | 畢 | 5 | 官 | 4 |
| 儀 | 8 | 該 | 7 | 被 | 6 | 船 | 5 | 幸 | 4 |
| 慶 | 8 | 慣 | 7 | 廊 | 6 | 報 | 5 | 怕 | 4 |
| 幫 | 8 | 旗 | 7 | 舒 | 6 | 象 | 5 | 於 | 4 |
| 鮮 | 8 | 福 | 7 | 媽 | 6 | 感 | 5 | 河 | 4 |
| 響 | 8 | 箏 | 7 | 煙 | 6 | 漢 | 5 | 肯 | 4 |
| 介 | 7 | 寬 | 7 | 農 | 6 | 管 | 5 | 段 | 4 |
| 任 | 7 | 熱 | 7 | 漂 | 6 | 綠 | 5 | 穿 | 4 |
| 早 | 7 | 輛 | 7 | 樂 | 6 | 德 | 5 | 苦 | 4 |
| 米 | 7 | 燒 | 7 | 熟 | 6 | 徵 | 5 | 飛 | 4 |
| 色 | 7 | 隨 | 7 | 據 | 6 | 樹 | 5 | 哪 | 4 |
| 衣 | 7 | 應 | 7 | 橋 | 6 | 頭 | 5 | 拿 | 4 |
| 男 | 7 | 懂 | 7 | 環 | 6 | 題 | 5 | 格 | 4 |
| 往 | 7 | 簡 | 7 | 士 | 6 | 手 | 5 | 祝 | 4 |
| 昆 | 7 | 難 | 7 | 升 | 5 | 仗 | 4 | 基 | 4 |

# 附錄二 本書用詞索引

本書將前述常用 500 常用字加以組合後，整理出下列約 400 餘個常用詞，按照筆劃數排列，字後的數字代表該詞在本書中出現的頁數。

一代人, 230, 235
一百萬, 108, 113
一個半小時, 122, 128
一般, 8, 16
一部分, 27, 33
一群一群, 7, 15
一對對, 167, 172
一邊…一邊…, 122, 128
了解, 44, 51
人口, 9, 16
人工湖, 45, 51
人民, 60, 69
人民大會堂, 8, 16
人生在世, 94, 99
人物, 7, 15
人家, 151, 157
人群, 8, 16
人牆, 94, 99
八十年代, 183, 189
三八婦女節, 135, 138
三五成群, 164, 167, 168
三輪車, 152, 158

下山, 7, 15
下棋, 167, 172
上天, 200, 205
上班, 183, 189
口味, 79, 85
口音, 230, 235
口頭語, 230, 235
士兵, 60, 66, 69
大人物, 43, 50
大不一樣, 9, 16
大戶人家, 152, 157
大多數, 40, 43, 47, 50
大約, 118, 122, 128
大理石, 93, 99
大街, 8, 16
大樓, 8, 16
不要說, 22, 26, 28, 32
不能沒有, 200, 206
不僅…而且…, 230, 235
中國美術館, 107, 113
中間, 27, 33
中飯, 122, 128

五四新文化運動, 44, 51
介紹, 79, 84
元旦, 134, 138, 140, 143
元首, 7, 15
元宵, 79, 84
公里, 94, 99
公務, 178, 183, 184, 189
分公司, 246, 251
分店, 246, 251
午門, 57, 61, 66, 70
升旗, 2, 7, 11, 15
升學壓力, 122, 128
反而, 148, 152, 154, 157
天安門, 1, 6, 10, 14
天壇, 5, 9, 14, 16
少數人, 44, 50
少數民族, 79, 84
引以為榮, 230, 235
心情, 167, 172
手下, 27, 33
手提, 246, 251
文物, 8, 16

方式, 108, 113
日子, 8, 16
日常, 44, 51
比薩餅, 246, 251
火車, 40, 44, 47, 50
王府井, 104, 109, 112
世界性, 138, 143
出了, 45, 51
出租車, 183, 189
出路, 122, 128
加上, 138, 143
包括, 26, 32
北京, 2, 6, 10, 14
半夜, 138, 143
卡車, 183, 189
去掉, 41, 44, 48, 51
可口, 215, 220
可惜, 45, 51
古代, 43, 50
古漢語, 44, 51
叫賣, 79, 84
台子, 200, 205
四分之三, 93, 99
四合院, 151, 157
四面八方, 7, 15
四處, 8, 16
外地, 152, 158
奶奶, 138, 143
尼克松, 92, 94, 97, 99
左右前後, 60, 70
市場, 107, 113
布什, 94, 99
平民, 60, 70
平房, 151, 157
必須, 26, 33
打仗, 26, 33
打牌, 167, 172
正陽門, 8, 16
民主, 44, 51

民用, 215, 220
民族, 76, 78, 84
民間, 79, 84
生產, 246, 251
用處, 183, 189
白話文, 45, 51
石船, 93, 99
石頭, 94, 99
立交橋, 245, 251
乒乓球, 123, 128
交通工具, 183, 189
全國, 62, 71
全新, 183, 189
划船, 138, 143
各方, 75, 78, 82, 84
各式各樣, 167, 172
名不見經傳, 107, 113
合理, 215, 220
吃法, 78, 84
吃的文化, 199, 200, 204
地下, 8, 16
地震, 200, 205
地鐵, 8, 16
多半, 152, 157
好奇, 246, 251
好處, 108, 113
好幾天, 62, 71
年代, 78, 84
成千上萬, 62, 71, 135,
成立, 215, 220
成交, 215, 220
成為, 45, 51
收入, 215, 220
收成, 200, 205
有意思, 152, 158
有趣, 61, 70
百科全書, 152, 157
羊肉, 167, 172
老外, 229, 230, 234, 235

老百姓, 27, 33
老是, 78, 84
考上, 122, 128
自行車, 167, 172, 177
行為, 230, 235
行業, 183, 189
西郊, 45, 51
西藥, 40, 44, 47, 50
位于, 96, 99
住房, 151, 157
努力, 122, 128
壯觀, 8, 16
希望, 215, 220
快餐, 138, 143
決定, 9, 16
男朋友, 123, 128
辛苦, 44, 50
事物, 44, 50
京劇, 21, 32, 165, 170
來比, 27, 33
來賓, 8, 16
來臨, 167, 172
兒童節, 138, 143
其中, 118, 122, 128,
其實, 40, 43, 46, 50
味道, 75, 78, 81, 84
咖啡店, 27, 33
周末, 177, 183, 184, 189
夜市, 167, 172
奇觀, 7, 15
幸運者, 122, 128
往往, 43, 50
放風箏, 8, 16
昆明湖, 90, 93, 95, 99
東西南北, 78, 84
炒菜, 78, 84
物力, 9, 16
知識, 45, 51
社會福利, 215, 220

## 附錄二 本書用詞索引

肯德基, 246, 251
花費, 91, 94, 97, 99
花錢, 43, 50
表演, 26, 32
迎接, 138, 143
近代, 108, 113
金水橋, 6, 15
長安街, 8, 16, 242, 247
長廊, 94, 99
長隊, 246, 251
門樓, 94, 99
信息, 122, 128
便宜, 108, 113
保護, 6, 15
俄羅斯, 215, 220
前門, 152, 157
前總統, 94, 99
城市, 94, 99
城門, 6, 15
客廳, 152, 157
建校, 45, 51
建造, 91, 94, 97, 99
建築群, 6, 15
怎麼辦, 200, 205
拜訪, 178, 183, 184, 189
指定, 123, 128
挑毛病, 215, 220
政府, 7, 15, 135, 141
故宮, 2, 10, 55, 64
故意, 213, 215, 217, 220
星期天, 122, 128, 134
流水, 108, 113
流行, 230, 235
流行語, 230, 235
流動, 230, 235
洗衣服, 196, 200, 201
活動, 3, 7, 11, 15
炸雞, 243, 246, 249, 251
甚至, 135, 138, 140, 143

皇后, 60, 69
皇帝, 6, 15
皇家, 43, 50
皇宮, 7, 15
相信, 167, 172
看來, 25, 27, 32, 33
紅葉, 200, 205
背書, 122, 128
背靠背, 152, 157
胡同, 152, 157
郊外, 200, 205
重視, 45, 51
降旗, 7, 15
面向, 152, 157
面對面, 149, 152, 154
風格, 22, 26, 28, 32
首都, 6, 14
香山, 200, 205
借光, 228, 230, 234, 235
個體戶, 215, 220
夏宮, 93, 99
家庭, 43, 50
家庭作業, 122, 128
旅遊, 108, 113
時期, 45, 51
時間, 44, 50
書本, 44, 51
書報, 183, 189
校園, 42, 45, 49, 51
氣球, 7, 15
消遣, 167, 172
海鮮, 78, 84
烤鴨, 78, 84
特色, 78, 84
狼煙, 91, 94, 96, 99
班主任, 123, 128
秦始皇, 58, 62, 67, 70
秦國, 62, 70
航空公司, 215, 220

茶水, 27, 31, 33,
茶話會, 138, 143
茶館, 27, 33
討價, 215, 220
退休, 152, 158
酒店, 167, 172
高處, 94, 99
鬼市, 164, 167, 168, 172
做人, 44, 50
做事, 44, 50
做官, 43, 50
做廣告, 167, 172
動物園, 138, 143
參觀, 4, 8, 12, 16
商業中心, 108, 113
國旗, 3, 7, 11, 15
國際, 78, 84
國際機場, 245, 251
國慶節, 7, 15
國營商店, 215, 220
將來, 43, 50
彩色電視, 246, 251
從那以後, 3, 11, 42, 59
接受, 43, 50
教育, 40, 43, 46, 50
晚會, 138, 143
殺掉, 61, 70
現代, 7, 15
現代歌, 27, 33
異性朋友, 123, 128
統一, 62, 70
習慣, 44, 51
處理, 60, 69
訪問, 60, 70
這場, 62, 71
麥當勞, 106, 108, 112
麻辣, 78, 84
最窄, 152, 157
勞動節, 138, 143

勞駕, 228, 230, 234, 235
博物院, 63, 71
博物館, 8, 16
報告, 61, 70
帽子, 107, 113
幾乎, 167, 172
幾米長, 8, 16
普通, 152, 158
曾經, 107, 113
無用, 44, 51
發展, 27, 33
稀有, 63, 71
等候, 7, 15
舒服, 60, 69
華里, 107, 113
街道, 79, 84
象徵, 6, 14
貴重, 63, 71
進出, 61, 70
郵局, 178, 183, 184
郵差, 183, 189
開放, 27, 33
開發, 245, 251
順利, 122, 128
順便, 179, 183, 186
黑白電視, 246, 251
傳統, 27, 33
意大利, 246, 251
感謝, 61, 70
想像, 246, 251
愛護, 26, 33
新鮮, 215, 220
暖和, 138, 143
業務, 108, 113
爺爺, 138, 143
當時, 44, 51, 104, 110
經過, 8, 16
經濟, 245, 251
羨慕, 183, 189

路燈, 167, 172
路邊, 78, 84
跳舞, 167, 172
農民, 43, 50
運動, 44, 50
遊覽, 7, 15
過夜, 200, 206
電視, 106, 108, 111
電腦, 123, 128
電話, 246, 251
圖畫, 151, 157
歌唱, 26, 32
歌劇, 26, 32
漢堡, 246, 251
福氣, 79, 84
種田, 43, 50
粽子, 79, 84
緊張, 123, 128
認出, 183, 189
遠處, 91, 94, 96, 99
儀式, 2, 7, 11, 15
儀器, 200, 205
劇院, 27, 33
廚房, 152, 157
廣場, 6, 15
德國, 245, 251
慶祝, 7, 15
數不清, 152, 158
樓房, 147, 151, 153
樂趣, 167, 172
熟悉, 122, 128
熟讀, 122, 128
熱鬧, 27, 33
蔬菜, 212, 215, 220
複習, 122, 128
談天, 24, 30, 199, 204
談天說地, 230, 235
課外活動, 123, 128
輪子, 183, 189

鬧意見, 123, 128
學問, 44, 51
據統計, 181, 183
據說, 58, 62, 75, 81
整個, 62, 70
歷史文物, 152, 158
燈市, 107, 113
磚頭, 152, 157
親眼, 4, 8, 12, 16
諮詢, 215, 220
辦公大樓, 246, 251
辦事, 93, 98
辦理, 183, 189
隨時, 245, 251
頤和園, 9, 16, 42, 49
環城公路, 245, 251
環繞, 5, 8, 13, 16
聲音, 27, 33
舉行, 7, 15
講話, 8, 16
還價, 212, 215, 217
鮮花, 7, 15
職業, 215, 220
雜誌, 183, 189
壞事, 62, 71
藝術, 26, 32
關于, 33,
關門, 60, 70
關係, 27, 33
願意, 93, 98
籃球, 122, 128
麵食, 78, 84
護城河, 6, 15
鐵道, 4, 8, 13, 16
變心, 27, 33
讓路, 230, 235
觀念, 44, 50
觀看, 7

# 20% Off
## or More ?

　　BIGI 公司是一家從事中文學習教材的出版公司，我們將提供您一系列學習中文的的教材，在我們公司所出版的書中您將感受到高品質的中文圖書。

　　只要填好下列表格，我們公司將在每一本新書問世前，主動提供一個給您"嚐鮮"的機會，您可以用意想不到的折扣，買到新書！

### 機會不多，只有一萬個名額。

您也可以在 Internet 上按照我們的問題，直接填表寄回。
（http://www.bigiintl.com　　E-mail: bigiintl@sprintmail.com ）

### BIGI 讀者俱樂部申請表

| Name | |
|---|---|
| Address | |
| Tel〔day〕 | Tel〔night〕 |
| Fax | |
| E-mail | |
| Please write down below if **you are a Chinese teacher?** ||
| School Name | |
| School Address | |
| School phone | |